Praise for

THE ABUNDANCE C

"Have you ever wondered why money and success seem to come so easily to some people when they have no more talent and no more skill than you, and they certainly don't work any harder than you do? Have you ever thought that you just didn't have the knack for making money or you just don't have 'money luck'? Here's the truth: Your level of success is a direct result of your mental programming about money and success—and you had that programming subconsciously installed years ago by parents, siblings, and friends. And if you're like most people, that money programming is holding you back. **The Abundance Code** *will peel back the layers of that faulty mental programming, and it will install the new success source code that will unconsciously and automatically put more abundance in your life."*

— **Jeff Walker,** #1 *New York Times* best-selling author of *Launch*

"If you don't update your computer software, your computer will begin to run more slowly, have more problems, and eventually stop working altogether. It's the same with your money beliefs and unconscious wealth 'software.' The beliefs that got you to this point in your life are probably not the ones that will take you where you long to be. **The Abundance Code** *is a chance to update your money and wealth beliefs and find financial freedom and more free time in your life. Julie Ann Cairns is a compassionate guide to rebooting your beliefs to reach your dream life."*

— **Bill O'Hanlon,** featured Oprah guest and author of more 35 books, including *Do One Thing Different* and *The Change Your Life Book*

"Julie Ann Cairns has written a book with a message I wish more intelligent, hardworking people would take to heart: Financial freedom and opportunity are within your reach. Beginning with her own personal story and incorporating insights from the fields of psychology, neuroscience, and economics, Julie Ann outlines detailed steps for overcoming the beliefs that keep so many from achieving their financial goals."

— **Ruth Buczynski, Ph.D.,** licensed psychologist and president, the National Institute for the Clinical Application of Behavioral Medicine

"**The Abundance Code** *is like having a guide shine a light on the hidden gates that lock you out from living the life you've dreamed of. Not only that, Julie Ann Cairns also hands you a set of keys to open each door. The only question is, are you ready to walk through? If so, be prepared to read and think, 'I don't do that. Oh my goodness . . . yes, I do.' As each myth is explained, you'll start to realize the obstacles are in your mind.* **The Abundance Code** *shows you the way out to a stunning new world of abundance.*"

— **Victoria Labalme**, international speaker, performing artist, and strategic performance coach

"*This is the type of education that should be mandatory in the world's school systems. Julie Ann Cairns's* **The Abundance Code** *is not only filled with true secrets to educate you on how to become more abundant, but also with actionable steps to get you there. Reading it, I could feel my beliefs on wealth strengthen. This is a must-read for anyone looking to have more abundance in their life. I know it will go into my library as a book that I need to read again and again to maintain my beliefs, and to live the Abundance Code.*"

— **J. B. Glossinger, Ph.D.**, CEO and founder, Morning Coach

"*Julie Ann Cairns is not only one of the most insightful, heart-based entrepreneurs I've met in my 30 years in business, but she is also uniquely qualified to bust all of our myths about money. Her riches to rags and back again story is a unique journey—and thank goodness she has decided to share it with the world.*

There is a new life lesson on every page of this book. My own belief was that 'money changes everything' in so many contexts: conversations, business deals, personal interactions, and so on. But after reading **The Abundance Code,** *I now see that it is a myth. It's not the money that changes everything; rather, it is how we get in touch in a profound way with our core desires, knowledge, and beliefs that has such an impact I will sleep better for the rest of my life having read this book and knowing that I am the one in full control when it comes to my relationship to money.*

By following Julie Ann's message closely and taking advantage of the hands-on tools in this book, I guarantee that you will have one epiphany after another as you, too, bust your own money myths."

— **Brian Kurtz**, former executive vice president, Boardroom, Inc., and serial direct marketer

THE
ABUNDANCE
CODE

HAY HOUSE TITLES OF RELATED INTEREST

YOU CAN HEAL YOUR LIFE, the movie, starring Louise Hay & Friends
(available as a 1-DVD program and an expanded 2-DVD set)
Watch the trailer at: www.LouiseHayMovie.com

THE SHIFT, the movie,
starring Dr. Wayne W. Dyer
(available as a 1-DVD program and an expanded 2-DVD set)
Watch the trailer at: www.DyerMovie.com

IF YOU CAN SEE IT, YOU CAN BE IT:
12 Street-Smart Recipes for Success,
by Jeff Henderson

INNER VOICE:
Unlock Your Purpose and Passion,
by Russ Whitney

MONEY MAGNET MIND-SET:
Tools to Keep You and Your Money on Track,
by Marie-Claire Carlyle

NLP: How to Use Neuro-Linguistic Programming to Change Your Life,
by Ali Campbell

THE WEALTH CHEF:
Recipes to Make Your Money Work Hard, So You Don't Have To,
by Ann Wilson

THE
ABUNDANCE
CODE

How to Bust the
7 Money Myths
for a Rich Life Now

JULIE ANN CAIRNS

HAY HOUSE, INC.
Carlsbad, California • New York City
London • Sydney • Johannesburg
Vancouver • Hong Kong • New Delhi

Cover design: Tiam Whitfield • *Interior design:* Pamela Homan

Simple versus Compound Growth graph (pg. 115): Courtesy of the author

Maslow's Illustration (pg. 151): Abraham Maslow © 1943, 1954

Chart (pg. 167): Springer and Kluwer Academic Publishers, *Social Indicators Research,*
Vol.40, Issue 1-2, 1997, pg. 189-216, "Measuring Quality of Life: Economic, Social,
and Subjective Indicators," by Ed Diener and Eunkook Suh, Figure 1: Economic
Quality of Life Compared to a Social Indicator Index, © 1997. With kind permission
from Springer Science and Business Media.

Chart (pg. 171): • Michael I Norton, Dan Ariely, *Perspectives on Psychological Science,* 6 (1) •
pp. 9-12, © 2011 The Authors • Reprinted by Permission of SAGE Publications

Library of Congress Cataloging-in-Publication Data

Cairns, Julie Ann, date.
 The abundance code : how to bust the 7 money myths for a rich life now / Julie Ann
Cairns.
  pages cm
 ISBN 978-1-4019-4728-6 (paperback)
 1. Wealth--Psychological aspects. 2. Finance, Personal--Psychological aspects. 3.
Financial security--Psychological aspects. 4. Wealth--Case studies. 5. Finance, Per-
sonal--Case studies. 6. Financial security--Case studies. I. Title.
 HB251.C224 2015
 332.024'01--dc23

                          2014049061

Tradepaper ISBN: 978-1-4019-4728-6
10 9 8 7 6 5 4 3 2 1
1st edition, September 2015

Printed in the United States of America

SUSTAINABLE
FORESTRY
INITIATIVE
Certified Chain of Custody
Promoting Sustainable Forestry
www.sfiprogram.org
SFI-01268
SFI label applies to the text stock

For Amma,
my beloved teacher,
mentor,
and guide

CONTENTS

INTRODUCTION

Do you want the freedom to choose the kind of work you do? Do you want the freedom to work less if you want to?

Do you want to make more money for less time and effort? Would you like to be able to work from home? Would you like to choose your own hours?

Would you rather do things just because you want to and not because you have to in order to pay the rent or the mortgage? Would you like to take more holidays or spend more time with your family?

Do you want to be able to retire early?

Do you want to be financially free?

If you answered yes to any of these questions, do you know how you can achieve those things?

Maybe you're thinking that if you knew how to have all of the above, then you would probably already have them! You would already have your dream home, you would already be spending your days doing the things you love to do, and you would already be able to travel or go on amazing adventures whenever you want.

So the biggest question is, What does it take to achieve the goal of financial freedom and abundance in your life?

Well, first of all, you need to really want whatever it is that you said yes to. That is, you need the *Desire*. You also need the know-how in order to get what you want. That is, you need the *Knowledge*. And finally, in order to be able to conquer all obstacles on the path and be successful, you need the courage of your convictions. That is, you need the *Belief*.

Without the vital ingredient of *Belief,* no amount of *Desire* or *Knowledge* can bear fruit.

Why is that? Because your subconscious beliefs are the essential inner code that will unlock true abundance for you in all areas of your life: wealth, success, and happiness. Your subconscious beliefs are what represent your own personal *Abundance Code.*

Either you are currently programmed subconsciously for abundance, wealth, success, and freedom, or you're not. If you are subconsciously programmed for it, then you'll already have it. If you're not, then you won't. It's as simple as that.

But if you don't already have the abundance you desire, don't despair. The *great* news is that if you're not currently programmed for abundance, you can change that. You can install your own *Abundance Code* in your subconscious mind right now, relatively quickly and easily. It's kind of like a mental software update—and that's exactly what I'm going to show you how to do in this book.

The truth is that everything you want, everything you desire, will come to you *only* once you have the right subconscious coding in place. Now, that's a bold statement, I know.

You're probably thinking, *Are you sure? That doesn't sound right! What about knowledge? What about effort? Isn't that enough?*

Yes, I'm sure. I've seen it over and over again. Knowledge and effort are not enough. You also need a supportive set of subconscious beliefs in place if you really want to succeed. I'm going to spend the rest of this book backing that idea up with a discussion of some key insights from the fields of psychology, neuroscience, and even economics, as well as practical case studies.

Let me be clear—I'm not saying that knowledge isn't important. It is. And so is effort. What I *am* saying is that if you don't also have the support of your subconscious beliefs, then you will remain frustrated in your efforts to succeed, no matter how much knowledge you have or how much effort you put in.

Right now, I just want you to open your mind to these two key ideas:

1. When you truly believe that you can have what you desire and—this is important—that you *deserve* it, then you simply won't accept anything less.

You will use all your knowledge, all your energy, and all your passion in the relentless pursuit of your goal. Even if you experience some setbacks along the way, you will learn from your mistakes, and your belief will continue to spur you on toward attaining your goal.

You will not give up, because you'll truly believe that you *can* achieve the goal. And simply because of that, you will be successful in the end.

2. When you *don't* have supportive beliefs about money and success, none of this is possible.

Without the right beliefs, you will give up at the first pothole along the road. Even if you have the right knowledge, you'll find you won't have the staying power needed to apply it successfully. Or you may try and try to achieve your desires, yet for some reason unknown to you, time and again you do not succeed. These kinds of frustrations should be red flags for you, and I'll explain why.

Without the right beliefs—a supportive set of subconscious codes that align with your conscious desires—you will actually sabotage your own success so that your outward experience of life does not contradict your inwardly held beliefs.

At this stage you may be thinking, *Excellent! I'm cool then. I'm pretty sure my beliefs are just fine. I definitely think that I can have what I want . . . I mean, why else would I go to so much effort to get the things I want if I didn't believe I could have them?*

Good point! Only . . . there's a flaw in that logic. Just because you think you want something, that doesn't mean you really *believe* you can have it on a deep, subconscious level.

Actually achieving your conscious desire might violate some deep-seated subconscious belief, creating a conflict and causing you to do things (without even realizing it) that have the effect of undoing your conscious efforts.

This is called subconscious sabotage, and I'll go into more detail about how it can work against you in Chapter 2. The funny thing is, just because you expend effort and try to get something, that doesn't mean you will let yourself succeed. Your conscious desires and your subconscious beliefs are not always in alignment. And when those two things are out of whack, well, that's a formula for frustration. Really—it's an actual formula, and I'll share that with you in Chapter 2 as well.

But first let's talk about the nasty truth: Most of us have inherited several core limiting beliefs about money that are actually *stopping* us from attaining wealth—no matter how much we may want that abundance or how hard we may be working toward getting it. I call these limiting beliefs the *7 Money Myths*.

Beware the 7 Money Myths

I'll tell you how I identified these core beliefs later on, but essentially, the 7 Money Myths are beliefs that have been passed down from generation to generation in the working and middle classes. They are so pervasive that they've become part of most people's subconscious programming.

The myths may vary slightly for each of us depending on our social, cultural, and religious backgrounds. But in the working and middle classes of Western societies, many of these beliefs are widespread.

The 7 Money Myths are beliefs about wealth, work, and money that have been presented to us in many ways throughout our lives—reinforced by family members, friends, the education system, employers, the media—and that's why so many of us have come to accept them at the subconscious level. They have become a part of the way we view the world, and we have taken them on hook, line, and sinker.

You can think of the 7 Money Myths collectively as your subconscious *poor programs*—they are the mental programs that are holding you back from experiencing a life of abundant wealth and freedom. They are subconscious blockages that are keeping you from living the rich, amazing, and inspiring life full of choice that you deserve to live. If what you want is a life of abundance, these beliefs are *not* helping you.

You probably have some, if not all, of the 7 Money Myths rattling around in your subconscious mind. They were installed there before you even really knew what was going on. And they are probably still lurking there like some kind of computer virus, stopping you from attaining the very things you most desire.

For those of us who have been on the receiving end of this powerful conditioning, it can be difficult to rise above it—even if we want to! How has this happened? Who on earth did this to us? And *why?*

Well, I'm not talking about any kind of conspiracy. These myths are not propaganda designed and spread by some secret society. You haven't been programmed with evil intent . . . at least, I don't think so. In fact, I think it all happened quite innocently.

Everyone has beliefs about wealth, work, success, and money—ideas that we were conditioned to accept as truth. The common sayings we heard over and over again while growing up represent hand-me-down beliefs about money, about life, and about relationships—"truths" that our ancestors believed and probably thought would protect us from pain, harm, or disappointment in life. They include statements like these:

- "Money doesn't grow on trees."
- "You have to work hard for your money."
- "Waste not, want not."
- "Easy come, easy go."
- "Money in, money out."
- "It takes money to make money."
- "The rich get richer while the poor get poorer."
- "Time is money."
- "Money won't make you happy."
- "There's more to life than money."

- "Money can't buy you love."
- "Money is the root of all evil."

Are any of these familiar? Didn't you hear sayings like these repeated many times as you were growing up?

The problem is, things that might have helped ensure your survival hundreds of years ago in different societal structures and class systems are not necessarily serving you so well anymore. In fact, these beliefs may be keeping you poor. The world has moved on, and so should you.

It's time to perform a mental software update and overwrite your subconscious poor programs. This update is pretty urgent actually, if what you want is a life of abundant wealth, freedom, and choice. You need to overwrite your subconscious poor programs with a much better alternative: your *Abundance Code.* This is a set of subconscious beliefs about money, wealth, and success that will support and not thwart the fulfillment of your conscious desires.

The Nautilus shell, represented on the cover of this book, is the sacred geometric symbol of expansion and growth—and a paramount code governing much of nature. Through cracking the code of the Nautilus, a startling fundamental mathematical mystery was revealed. Just like the Nautilus, this book will crack the *Abundance Code* by busting the most prevalent, destructive money myths in existence. Unless you perform this subconscious programming update, you will likely continue to be frustrated in achieving your desires in life. So do stick around, because what I have to share with you could change your life and your financial future *forever.*

Why Did I Write This Book, and Why Should You Read It?

I've come to see my life journey with respect to money as a great blessing. I have a unique perspective that comes from an unusually broad range of experiences regarding money.

I finally feel that I have achieved many of my goals—of financial freedom, of real friendships, of a sense of belonging with a group of like-minded people—but I will admit to you that my journey with money and wealth, stretching from childhood to now, hasn't always felt like an easy ride. Part of the reason I wanted to write this book is because I'd like it to be a whole lot easier for you than it was for me.

As you'll discover, my journey has had a lot of ups and downs, but it got me to where I am today, and I am very grateful. There is a lot of bounty in my life on so many levels, including financially. And if I can help you get to your goal of financial freedom faster and more directly because of what I am able to share with you from my experience, by giving you my shortcut blueprint for rewiring your beliefs about money and stopping internal sabotage forever, then I will be *really* happy. That would be the icing on the cake for me.

The purpose of this book is to challenge some of your inherited beliefs about money and expose them for what they really are: *myths*. For many, this is the first step in changing the mind on a deeper level.

Next, you'll need to make some decisions about what you would rather believe. What kind of beliefs will support you and provide the nutrient-rich soil that will allow endless possibility to take root in your life? How will you write your *Abundance Code*? We will talk about that, too.

Changing your underlying programming is critically important in manifesting a different reality. And if you really want to change your belief structure, you have to not only weaken the old beliefs, but also replace them with new ones. You'll need to identify a new set of beliefs that better supports your quest for financial freedom and actively work to install it.

If you don't do this essential belief-change work, you may find yourself thwarted at every turn in your quest for financial freedom. I will provide you with a blueprint for making these essential belief changes later on in the book.

I call the seven limiting belief programs that I identified "myths" because they aren't really true. They are not facts. They do not have to be true for me, and they do not have to be true for you either. Yet they are commonly held to be true by most people on a subconscious level. They form part of our collective programming.

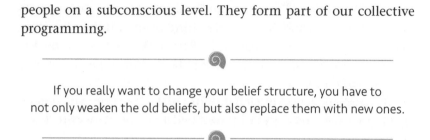

If you really want to change your belief structure, you have to not only weaken the old beliefs, but also replace them with new ones.

Let me ask you: Wouldn't you rather be experiencing a reality where you don't have to work hard for your money? Would you like a reality where money comes into your life easily, where your wealth continues to grow, and where money facilitates your happiness and your sense of well-being? Which will it be—the reality you were conditioned to accept, or the one you actively and imaginatively create for yourself?

It's time to start *busting* the money myths you have bought into for so long and to begin the process of building a new code. The myths have been holding you back from the life of abundance you deserve, and it's time to change that. So let's get on to it, right here, right now!

The Content and Structure of This Book

I'm going to take a very pragmatic approach and look at issues that are of real-life, practical importance. There are four crucial questions that we need to address over the course of the book:

1. What are the most common beliefs about money?

2. Where have they come from?

3. How do they manifest in daily life?

4. How can they be changed?

As for the structure of this book: First, I'll share with you some of my own background and why I got interested in this topic in the first place. I'll go into depth about my personal experiences, education, and work, because I want you to comprehend clearly how much I understand this topic from every angle. I truly have been there!

Then I'm going to talk about the cognitive framework that we humans have evolved over time, which has ensured that our subconscious beliefs are such powerful drivers of our behavior. I'm going to discuss how and why your beliefs shape the way in which you see the world.

Next, I'm going to dissect the most common beliefs about money: the 7 Money Myths. I'm going to take them apart one by one, including practical examples and case studies from real people, so that you can easily see how these or similar belief patterns may be showing up in your own life.

At the end of each chapter you'll find a section called "Digging Deep," which will provide questions to help you get to the bottom of how the chapter topic is at work in your life. You can write out your thoughts in a journal, discuss them with a friend or in a group, or just spend some time thinking about the issues at play. These questions are followed by "Action Steps," so you can start to integrate the ideas that are being presented to you right away into your daily life.

And finally, I'm going to give you practical exercises you can use to change your existing limiting beliefs. I will show you how you can replace your old beliefs with new beliefs that will support you and propel you, like a jet-powered rocket pack, toward financial freedom.

There may be some things in life you can't control, but you *are* in control of what you choose to believe. And trust me when I say there is *enormous* power in that.

Digging Deep

1. What were some of the common sayings about money introduced to you by your parents, teachers, or peers when you were growing up?

2. Do you ever notice yourself repeating similar sayings in your day-to-day conversations? If you're a parent, for example, do you ever repeat those kinds of things to your kids? Do you say them to your friends?

3. When you reflect on your life, do you feel that your beliefs about money have affected the types of decisions you've made? For example, if you believe that "money doesn't grow on trees," does it mean that you are cautious with your money? Do you budget and save? Or are you more "easy come, easy go"?

Action Steps

1. Do a "brain dump" of all the sayings about money you've heard throughout your life. At this stage, don't worry about whether you might believe them; just write them all down.

2. Look at the list and spend some time contemplating each item. If you did believe the things on the list, would those beliefs help you or hinder you in achieving your goals in life?

3. If you see an item on the list that you suspect is not a helpful belief for you to have, how could you rewrite that belief to make it more supportive of your goals?

CHAPTER ONE

My Story

From Riches to Rags . . . and Back Again

To help you understand my perspective and my experience with all the concepts in this book, I want to share my story with you. As you'll see, this book was born directly from my desire to share all I've learned with you.

Fortunate Beginnings

I was lucky enough to grow up in a prosperous family. Both my parents were born in Australia, which they left in their early 20s. After a stint in the U.K., they ended up immigrating to Canada.

My father was a highly respected oral and maxillofacial surgeon who also trained as an anesthesiologist. He used his dual specialist knowledge to pioneer new techniques in oral surgery sedation. He was also a major in the Canadian Army Reserve. Dad was a very busy man, and he worked very hard. He made good money, and with that money my parents made some excellent investments.

By the time I was eight years old, our family had everything we could want in terms of material prosperity. We moved to a country estate that was situated on a large plot of land on the shores of a beautiful lake. The house was my parents' dream home—architect designed and built exactly the way they wanted.

It was spacious, with a big wraparound entertaining deck that overlooked the lake. It had a huge open-plan living, dining, and kitchen area that ended up being featured in a magazine; vaulted ceilings and stone fireplaces; floor-to-ceiling windows capturing the magnificent view; an indoor, heated swimming pool; a sauna; a gym; four bedrooms; three bathrooms; a sunroom; a media room; and a bar. It was a big, beautiful, luxurious house.

My brother, sister, and I loved the lake house. In winter we skated on the lake, whizzed around on snowmobiles, and cross-country skied. We were also members of a nearby downhill ski club. In summer we swam in the crystal clear water, rode our bikes, and played endless games of hide-and-seek on the property. Happy days.

We all had expensive hobbies. My brother was a very good shot with a rifle, and his sports were hunting and skeet shooting. He usually got a new gun every Christmas . . . a gift that somehow didn't seem totally in keeping with the spirit of the holiday, if you ask me.

My sister and I were trained in equestrian riding. We spent a month each year at horse-riding camp, learning what I thought were somewhat useless skills, such as chasing after the scent of foxes on horseback, galloping alongside a pack of slobbering bloodhounds while trussed up in a uniform of red blazer with black velvet lapels, white cravat, riding pants, black velvet helmet, and shiny black leather boots. I liked the outfit a lot—the slobbering and barking of the hounds not so much!

My sister was the star equestrienne, so my parents bought her a pony, and she began competing in show jumping and dressage. Soon her bedroom became filled with trophies and blue ribbons. I was better at gymnastics. I began competing in that sport and spent around 20 hours per week training with a coach at a private gymnastics club. I also filled my room with trophies and medals.

Both Mum and Dad became qualified private pilots, and they bought two small airplanes (his and hers), which they kept in a hangar at a nearby airfield. On family holidays they would fly us all in one of the planes to wherever we were going: down to Florida or maybe New England, or up to cottage country.

So we had a great life, and we were very fortunate. My parents had achieved pretty much all their dreams, and for a while there they certainly seemed to be having a good time and enjoying life. They collected art, had lots of friends, held fabulous parties, spent a month each year vacationing somewhere exotic while all of us kids were at camp, and generally appeared to be having plenty of fun. Maybe too much fun . . .

Growing Awareness

It was the 1970s, and I guess it was a party decade. "Harvey Wallbangers"—that's what my mother drank. Dad was more of a beer, whisky, and cognac man. It seemed like everyone smoked. Mum liked some long, thin cigarettes. I remember the advertising slogan for them, paired with a picture of a glamorous woman holding a cigarette: "You've come a long way, baby," which I think was some sort of dubious referral to cigarette smoking as a symbol of women's liberation. Dad smoked Old Port cigarillos, which were like skinny cigars with white plastic tips that were supposed to have been dipped in port.

I remember the men wore a lot of striped trousers and weird polyester shirts. The women wore flowing chiffon and satin "lounge suits" and sported big hair (mainly wigs) and fake eyelashes.

There didn't seem to be much concern about having a few too many drinks and then driving home. And I don't really remember many people bothering to wear seat belts back then either. In fact, my mother (who had also briefly taken up race-car driving as a hobby) drove a zippy little red sports car, and I don't think it even *had* seat belts. I remember giggling in a mixture of fear and delight as I slid around unrestrained on the very small backseat.

Around the time we moved into the lake house, my brother, who was the eldest, was sent off to an exclusive private boarding school. Apparently, Prince Andrew went there briefly during a stint in the colonies. That fact (or fiction) was repeated a lot in our house.

My sister and I were deemed to be still too young for boarding school, so we were sent to the local primary school. My parents' dream house was in a rural area, and most of the people in that area were farming families that were nowhere near as wealthy as we were. This is how I first started to become aware of the fact that people have different attitudes about wealth.

My sister and I both experienced that it was very difficult to make friends at the local school. Once it became widely known who we were and which house we lived in (in a small community, that didn't take long), the other kids seemed to view us with a mixture of envy and suspicion. It became pretty clear, pretty quickly, that most of the kids didn't *want* to like us. The exceptions were a few who were nice initially, perhaps because they were angling for an invitation to see our house. Once they'd seen the place, though, they joined the others in being cold.

That was an interesting experience. I'm not putting it forward as some kind of sob story. I know we were very fortunate to have been so well-off. It's even possible that we acted in a way that was seen by others as snobby, although I don't remember ever having snobby feelings or intentions. I just wanted people to like me, and I was kind of perplexed about why they so clearly did not. But I caught on in the end, and the experience taught me about how money and wealth can represent an emotional trigger for a lot of people.

The Other Side

Then, as fate would have it, the shoe ended up on the other foot. When I was 11 years old, my parents broke up; and within two years of divorcing, somehow they were both flat broke.

My sister and I were taken by Mum from school one day and told to pack one suitcase each from home, and then she hid us from my dad for a few months. My brother was in boarding school at the time and didn't find out we had gone until months later. In the meantime, Dad was searching for us frantically and going out of his mind.

Mum was afraid of him, obviously, or she wouldn't have hidden us like that. I'd never seen Dad be violent toward her, and he'd never been violent toward us kids either, apart from dishing out the occasional run-of-the-mill spanking, which was the norm in that era. And to be fair, Mum was also known to brandish a wooden spoon for spankings from time to time. But I guess she was convinced that Dad was capable of being violent at that point.

So we left the fantastic lakefront mansion, and after a few months of being shunted around between different hiding spots, Mum moved with my sister and me into a scrubby old dive in a low-rent country town. I was enrolled in the local public school.

It was kind of a rough school, so it did seem as if half the kids wanted to beat the hell out of me . . . but to my surprise, the other half were actually very friendly. Soon I had plenty of friends—a whole *group* of friends—and we would hang out and do things together. This was a new experience for me, having a group of friends. I really liked it. It was fun, and I felt accepted. And it was a welcome counterpoint to all the trauma and drama that was going on in my family life.

I started to see a connection between having common financial circumstances and belonging. I began to believe that if your financial means are wildly different from those of your peers, it makes it difficult to be part of the club. This is a myth in itself, actually, and not something that I'm saying was particularly helpful to believe. It's just a belief I took on at the time.

Now, where all my parents' money went is a very good question. I feel as though that's really not my story to tell though . . . it's theirs. Furthermore, I don't even know the real deal! I've heard many garbled, twisted, and drunken accounts of it over the years, none of which make much sense.

Basically, by the time my parents broke up when I was 11, both of them had serious drinking problems. You could say that by that stage Dad was an alcoholic, and I'm pretty sure my mother was having some kind of paranoid nervous breakdown, also fueled by a lot of alcohol. So maybe a better question would be: How likely was it that they could have managed to keep their money when they were both unraveling mentally and emotionally?

Here's what I do know: My mother left my father for a lawyer (actually he was Dad's tax attorney). Things had been rocky between my parents for a while, so this guy was probably more of a catalyst than a cause. And she obviously loved him because they got married and are still together more than 30 years later. Of course, my father doesn't see it that way. His point of view is that it was the ultimate betrayal. Dad had invited this guy to move in with us for a few months because he was down on his luck, and when he got back on his feet and left, he took my mother with him.

Maybe the fact that this guy (who later became my stepfather) had previously been my father's tax lawyer had something to do with why Dad didn't seem to end up with much money in the divorce settlement. To be honest, though, I don't know. I'm just guessing that it was an unfortunate turn of events from Dad's perspective.

Under normal circumstances, being an attorney, my stepfather probably should have been a pretty good provider. I think that at least some of the money that Mum got in the settlement went toward buying my stepfather into a legal practice near Toronto. Again, I don't know for sure. But somehow he was installed in a practice, and we moved from our small-town life to a suburb close to the city.

Not long after moving there, my stepfather got disbarred, which meant that he could no longer practice law and lost his practice. Why? Well, once again, I'm in the dark. No one ever told me a credible story, and I was just a kid at the time.

I wish I had more facts to impart. However, I don't want to say something that's not right . . . and the truth about what really happened during those crazy tumultuous years in my family has been elusive. I've been told all kinds of conflicting things by the different people who were involved, and I've also heard different tales from the same people at different times. Who knows what to believe, so I'm trying to just stick to the things that I know for sure.

What I'm certain of is that my stepfather lost the right to work in his profession, and he spent the next 15 years or so unemployed. Shortly after that, my mother ended up declaring bankruptcy. It seemed all the money was gone.

Then, as if finances weren't strained enough, my mother and stepfather decided to have a baby. I'm glad they did—I love my little brother—but wow, money was tight.

Soon after my parents broke up, my sister had gone to live with my father, and they moved to Australia. My older brother saw out the year at boarding school, and then he ended up living with Mum, my stepfather, me, and our new baby brother.

Mum was the only one in the household who was working. First she got a job as a flying instructor, and then she tried selling insurance. After my little brother was born, she found something with more reliable hours and steadier pay: being the office manager in a dental practice. There were five mouths to feed in our house and only one not-so-large income. I honestly don't know how Mum managed to make ends meet.

This was all a huge lifestyle change for me. Before my parents split, I'd been accustomed to a life of privilege. After the divorce, my mother's bankruptcy, and my stepfather being disbarred, we really had no money to speak of at all.

That was a rude shock for me, to say the least. No more expensive equestrian training or show jumping. No more skiing. No more private gymnastics coaching. No more holidays at Disney World, having flown there in our own private airplane. No more of whatever I wanted, whenever I wanted it. It felt to me like losing a real-life game of *Snakes and Ladders*—as if I'd slid down to the bottom of the socioeconomic ladder in one roll of the dice.

The fact that our change in fortunes was a bummer is probably not surprising. It altered our lives drastically and made things much, much worse in so many ways.

There were some compensations though. As I said, having more friends was an unexpected upside to suddenly not having more money than my peer group. That was nice. But on the other hand, being so financially constrained, having radically fewer choices in life and much tougher living conditions . . . that was a major drag.

I remember deciding around the age of 15 that when I grew up, I wanted to have *both* financial freedom *and* plenty of quality friendships. I wanted to have the freedom and the wide range of choices that come with money, as well as a strong sense of belonging with a group of like-minded people. I wanted friendships based on common interests and shared mind-sets that were not necessarily predicated on common financial circumstances. I set my intention firmly on becoming my own definition of rich: a wealth of money, opportunities, choices, and wonderful friendships. I wanted all that, and I wanted it bad.

I had the burning desire. Next, I set out to get the knowledge.

Finding My Own Path

I studied hard at school. I moved from Canada to Australia to live with my dad at the age of 16 because I felt I'd have access to a better standard of education there.

I graduated high school with good scores and enrolled to study economics and statistics at university. I was a good student and I kept up my grades. University education was free in Australia back then, so I lucked out in that respect.

I was recruited by the Reserve Bank of Australia, Australia's central bank, when I finished my undergraduate degree. The bank was known as an institution that only interviewed those who'd been at the top of their cohort. Later, I won a prestigious scholarship from the Japanese government, one of only ten awarded per year across all disciplines, to study for a master's in finance and business administration in Japan. Back then, Japan was *the* dominant economic powerhouse in the world. Remember that?

I ended up spending four additional years at university in Japan studying various aspects of economics, statistics, finance, and the stock market; and I graduated at the top of my class. Some of my research was funded by a grant from Nomura Securities, one of the top broking firms in Japan. My thesis paper was titled "Pricing Anomalies in the Japanese Stock Market." I learned everything I could about money. And of course, I learned the Japanese language, too. I had to because all my classes were taught in Japanese.

I bought my first business while I lived in Japan, jointly with a business partner. It was an English school I ran on the side while I completed my studies. That experience taught me how to leverage my time and not just exchange my hours for dollars (a money myth that had been playing out in my life until that point—more on this in Chapter 4).

After I graduated with my master's, I returned to Australia to work at the Reserve Bank in their international financial markets and currency research department. I then went on to work in the funds management area of one of Australia's largest merchant banks, where I was an economic analyst and built statistical models for currency and fixed-interest trading. I became a highly skilled financial markets researcher and economic analyst. I also started to personally invest in property.

In 2002, I left my job in funds management and moved into the field of financial market trading education as co-owner of the Trading Pursuits Group, which my business partner and I founded in 2001. I've been with Trading Pursuits ever since, and I've continued to invest in real estate, the stock market, and entrepreneurial business ventures.

I had a strong desire to be wealthy, and I acquired a lot of knowledge relevant to that pursuit. One of the key things I've learned is the power of leverage. Over the years I've been an equity stakeholder in various businesses to leverage my time. I've also invested in real estate and the stock market in order to leverage my assets.

I focused all those years on having a plan for growing my wealth—what I thought was a good plan based on strong desire, a lot of knowledge, and experience. But as it turns out, desire is not enough. Knowledge is not enough either. Even experience can be overrated if you continue to have the same self-sabotage pop up again and again. And lo and behold, I was not exempt from that.

New Lessons

Although my partner and I had invested very well in real estate—at one point we had built up a portfolio of nearly 30 rental properties with a combined value of about $10 million—we then turned around and lost a lot of our real-estate wealth by investing in something we knew very little about: retail businesses.

We opened a chain of six flower shops (in partnership with a couple of other investors) and bought two Indian takeaway restaurants. On paper these both looked like great opportunities, but in hindsight we went in too heavy and didn't see the warning signs soon enough when things were not working out as planned. We also really didn't know what we were doing when it came to running retail businesses. The devil is in the details, as they say.

We learned a lot of important and painful lessons about business from losing all that money. For example, you have to really understand what your open-door costs are in retail business—that's how much it costs you to open the doors of your business each day, week, and month—and you have to budget enough of a cash buffer to cover those costs when sales are slow. Most retail businesses have physical overheads such as rents, staff wages, and food and stock that can spoil if it's not sold in time. In that sense, those businesses can bleed money . . . and fast!

We learned how important it was to read the fine print on contracts like leases for premises, equipment, and the like. If you don't negotiate well up front, you can be liable for lots of hidden charges and unexpected penalties if you decide to terminate the contract. We got burned a bit in that respect due to our lack of understanding.

Also, in a business like food or flowers, unless you have a good stock control system in place that lets you keep precise track of everything going into and out of the business, you run the risk of people essentially stealing from you. Having good stock control, accounting systems, and procedures is vital.

So yes, a lot of important lessons were learned. It was hard for us to see much of the wealth we had built up through our real-estate investing just bleed away through our own lack of knowledge and poor decision making, and because we had not taken proper control or precautions over important risk factors in our retail businesses. I have to say, though, that we ended up putting some of those lessons to good use in our trading-education business, so it was not a total washout when viewed from that perspective.

These days, I read all my contracts very carefully and I negotiate for better terms. Everything is tracked and documented, and I keep a careful eye on the cash flow in my business. I look deeply into the accounts and do a lot of financial forecasting about different scenarios that could impact the business, so I am as prepared as possible for future events.

Some lessons can be hard at the time they are being learned. However, I believe now that if I learn something valuable from an experience, then it becomes an asset for me. It becomes a stepping-stone to my future success. That's a positive and supportive belief that I have installed for myself.

But I didn't always have that belief, and sometimes in the past it was hard for me to not get discouraged. Financially, I've had many ups and downs. I've made and lost millions of dollars. I've made and lost friends, too. And sometimes those losses have really hurt.

For many years I was frustrated in my efforts to succeed—and I know I'm not alone.

My Epiphany

I work in the field of wealth creation, so I've interacted professionally with hundreds of people who were also striving to achieve financial freedom. Some have been successful; some have not. Some, like me, experienced repeated cycles of success and failure.

I've known wealthy people who've grown up with money, for whom wealth is an accepted and expected state of being. I've known poor people who've never had wealth and simply do not believe they ever would or could. And I've seen pretty much everything in between. I've also experienced most of those states of mind myself due to my own crazy roller-coaster ride with wealth.

The turning point for me came in 2008. Trading Pursuits Group was in trouble as a result of the global financial crisis. A couple of years earlier, my partner and I had borrowed money to expand the business. As a result, we had a significant amount of medium-term debt that just happened to be due to mature in December 2008.

The global financial markets crashed in October 2008. That was a scenario that I hadn't seen coming. I hadn't anticipated the extent of the crisis. I don't think many people had, nor the wide-ranging consequences of it.

For us, the consequences were harsh. We suddenly found that we could not refinance or roll over the company debt because of the bank credit squeeze that followed the crash. Banks were basically not lending any money to anyone. No funds were available from any bank in the world to refinance our debt.

We were staring down the barrel of bankruptcy. I had just taken over as managing director of the company, and that looked like it might be a very short-lived promotion!

What's more, it felt like an eerie repetition of my childhood family experience. And then it hit me—maybe it *was* a repetition of that. I was about the same age my parents had been when they'd lost everything. Could it be that I was re-creating that experience in my own adult life? Could it be that I somehow believed that was "normal"?

I'd lost plenty of money plenty of times before, but not since I was a child had I been so close to losing *everything*. It took coming to the brink for me to finally recognize the pattern, to trigger an epiphany. At last I saw the powerful effect that my subconscious beliefs were having on my life.

I'd been observing the symptoms of subconscious sabotage in my clients, family, and friends for years. But what's the old verse? *Why do you see the speck in your neighbor's eye, but do not notice the log in your own eye?* Somewhat arrogantly, I hadn't seen the same symptoms of sabotage in my own psyche—until I nearly lost it all. Only then did I wake up to the fact that I, too, was in a mental battle with my limiting subconscious beliefs, and they were winning! They were winning because . . . they always do.

Finally, I started to see how limited my own mental programming was regarding money, wealth, and success. I saw how and why that programming was causing such a fruitless and exhausting cycle of success and failure for me. I saw it . . . but I felt as though I was powerless to fight it.

Luckily, someone had previously recommended an excellent book called *The Power of Your Subconscious Mind* by Joseph Murphy, which I read many months before the crash. The book is a classic that was originally published in 1963, and the title pretty much sums it up. According to the author, every outer experience—good or bad—can be seen as a natural consequence of deeply held subconscious beliefs.

The book contained some practical exercises for overwriting subconscious beliefs, yet I hadn't used them. But when I found my back against the wall and was facing imminent financial ruin, I was willing to try anything. So I made a decision, a momentous decision, a decision that would change everything . . .

I decided *not* to fight. I decided to *overwrite.*

I questioned whether it could in fact be that easy. Could I actually change my outer experiences just by doing some simple exercises to overwrite key aspects of my subconscious programming? But I suspended my disbelief and decided to give it a try.

And—*boom!* It started to work.

The Power of Belief

Since then it's been, well, sometimes exhilarating and sometimes scary. A lot of change has happened for the better.

Once I was onto the idea that all real change comes from *within* my own subconscious mind, I did a lot more research on how to reprogram myself for success, health, abundance, emotional freedom, financial freedom, happiness—whatever I wanted. That's how I discovered my own *Abundance Code*. The secret to unlock wealth and prosperity lay in the proper programming of my subconscious mind.

I'm not claiming that I'm the first person in the world to figure out that the keys to outer success reside within. After all, as I said, Joseph Murphy published *The Power of Your Subconscious Mind* in 1963, before I was even born. And Napoleon Hill was onto it, too, when he wrote *Think and Grow Rich* in 1937. I'm sure there were many others even before him.

One thing I have noticed that is unique about my approach, however, is that I've identified *the 7 Money Myths* I mentioned earlier. This set of sequential subconscious barriers to abundance is blocking most people from achieving the life of abundant wealth and financial freedom that they deserve.

That's right: I've found that the 7 Money Myths are *sequential* internal mental barriers, kind of like gates. Because of that, they appear in a particular order in this book for a reason. By busting the myths, which is what this book shows you how to do, you will be able to discover a fast-track path to unlocking your own personal *Abundance Code*.

For me, some changes happened immediately after my big epiphany, at the beginning of my quest to reprogram my own subconscious mind for abundant wealth and success. This was because some subconscious blocks were very easy to clear. Others needed some soul-searching. The process was kind of like peeling an onion. Once I cleared one block, I would find another even more deeply held subconscious belief that was also a subtle obstacle to my conscious goals.

I've since learned many other techniques to help me change my subconscious beliefs, besides the ones covered in *The Power of Your Subconscious Mind*. I discovered that it was important to also shift my ingrained habits along with my beliefs in order to support my conscious goals for greater freedom and abundance. I'll expand more on this in Chapter 10.

Today my financial position is the strongest it's ever been, and it seems to be going from strength to strength. I've also been able to move away from drama in my relationships; to have stronger friendships based on mutual respect and support; to be a better friend, partner, and mother; to communicate more clearly; to have healthier boundaries; and to be more certain of the kind of life I want to live.

For me, the process of clearing the subconscious barriers to all of this wasn't entirely painless. I had to let go of programming that was no longer serving me, and sometimes that was hard. I needed to identify exactly what limiting beliefs I had taken on in my early development. At times there were tears and sorrow when I revisited painful memories and saw how I had coded those events into subconscious beliefs about the world.

There was a positive purpose in revisiting those dark days, though, because I knew I needed to uncover the limiting codes I had installed back then that were keeping me stuck in various replays of those patterns. Then, once I identified an unhelpful and limiting belief, I had to decide what I *wanted* to believe instead and take some basic steps to install the new beliefs.

Does that sound too vague? Don't worry; we'll address the process in a very practical way as we progress through the book, especially in Chapter 10. All you really need to know right now is the outcome: As soon as I began to update my mental software—to change my subconscious beliefs to be more in line with my conscious goals—*my life changed for the better very rapidly.*

The results were worth it. Oh yes. Amongst other things, our company finances turned around. It didn't happen overnight, and a lot of adjustments had to be made; but we avoided bankruptcy, we met all our debt repayment obligations, and we came out of it stronger than ever. Our business went from being millions of dollars in debt to debt free, with millions of dollars in cash in the bank, over a period of four short years. Our annual revenues nearly tripled during that time.

This stellar turnaround was not achieved in a favorable business environment. It was done during the four years immediately following the global financial crisis, when the economy was slow and many of our competitors went out of business. I look back on it, and I am still amazed. Beliefs are powerful things.

Living in a New Way

I've made a lot of progress in reprogramming my subconscious mind since then. It's an ongoing process. But the difference is that now I know what to do when I hit a blockage. When I uncover beliefs that do not serve me or what I want in life, I do the work to change them.

Will I ever be done? I don't know. I *do* know that subconscious sabotage is something to remain vigilant about. What I mean is that it's tricky to decide with any degree of confidence that we have completely vanquished all our subconscious limiting beliefs. They are *sub*conscious after all. It's always a good idea to remain aware and on the lookout for potential indications of when our underlying programs are not aligned with our conscious goals.

Also, conscious goals can change over time. What I wanted from life when I was in my 20s is not necessarily the same as what I want now. So in this way, I may continue to uncover subconscious blockages as my conscious goals in life shift. And that's okay.

How do I know that I have a block when it's below the level of my conscious awareness? Well, I find that one of the biggest indicators of misalignment is frustration. If your subconscious beliefs align with your conscious desires, then the attainment of your desires just flows naturally—unconsciously, even. It feels easy. When your beliefs and your desires are not in alignment, then nothing is easy. Everything is a struggle, and it seems like nothing flows.

When that's the kind of experience I'm having—one of frustration and a lack of flow—I know that I need to do some detective work. I need to contemplate what might be blocking me. Once I know what the block is (the pattern that I don't want to experience anymore and the belief that underlies it), then I need to get clear on what I *really do* want to experience instead and identify what kind of belief would support me in attaining that goal.

In this way, I'm evolving. I'm expressing and living an ever more fulfilled and purpose-driven life every day, in every way. My life just keeps on getting better and better as I systematically dismantle the subconscious obstacles to my success and happiness. As a result, the abundance I experience just keeps on getting more profound and stable.

That does not mean I don't encounter challenges and learning experiences like everyone else. I've had some truly crazy stuff happen over the years. But these days, I know that if there is something in my life that I would like to be better, then the *last* thing I should do is exhaust myself by trying and trying to change my outer circumstances.

I now know that I should first look inward to see where the internal subconscious blockage is within my own mind and understand why it is causing an unhelpful or unwanted pattern of outward experience. It's a very old idea: that we should look within for the real answers to our outward problems. The words above the entrance to the temple of the oracle at Delphi in Greece more than 2,500 years ago were *Gnothi seauton,* which translate as "Know thyself."

I have come to realize that these truly are words to live by on many levels. It's not just about finances. It's about having a fulfilling, abundant life of freedom and choice. And for that, a supportive set of subconscious beliefs is vital. Still, it can take me a while to wise up and see a persistent pattern of sabotage—like the 40-odd years it took me to reach my first big epiphany!

It Takes All the Right Ingredients to Bake a Cake

I'm not perfect, and my wealth journey has at times been a bumpy ride, but I've learned a lot along the way personally that I'll share with you in this book. I've also learned plenty of great lessons through coaching hundreds of clients and from observing their many different patterns of behavior.

The key insight I've gained over the years is that we all have biases when it comes to our decision-making processes. These biases are usually far from rational, and they are often self-sabotaging. After witnessing various behaviors in myself, my family members, my friends, and my clients, I've come to realize (as I described in my personal story) that the real driver of self-sabotaging behavior is rooted at the level of belief. Those who persistently don't succeed and are frustrated in their efforts—despite having a burning desire and all the knowledge they should need in order to do so—aren't succeeding because on a subconscious level they either *don't believe they could* or *don't believe they should.*

I discovered for myself that in order to succeed, *all* the right ingredients need to be in place:

- The right knowledge
- A strong desire to succeed
- Discipline
- Persistence
- Patience
- A willingness to make mistakes
- An ability to acknowledge mistakes quickly
- An inclination to learn from mistakes
- A willingness to try again
- The ability to feel comfortable with success, and to feel deserving of it
- *And* a supportive belief structure about myself, about money, and about success

I identified the set of common limiting belief programs about money that I call the 7 Money Myths. I started seeing these myths playing out everywhere. I came to realize that for me, for my family, for my friends, and for many of my clients, the 7 Money Myths were powerful subconscious programs that were blocking the path to achieving true and lasting financial freedom.

Once I saw these limiting beliefs clearly in myself, I was able to do the work to change my own inner programming to be more supportive of my outer goals. As I described, when I changed my beliefs, I found that my whole worldview and the way I experienced life changed, too. It was massive change for the better, and it happened really quickly.

As you move through the following chapters, you'll learn more about the 7 Money Myths and how they may be affecting your life. It's my hope that your journey to abundance will be smoother than mine, and this book will help you get there!

Digging Deep

1. Write down your own personal and family history with respect to money and wealth. What were the financial circumstances of your family? What did that teach you? Think back on your life . . . Have you experienced ups and downs with respect to money? What happened?

2. Compare your childhood experiences regarding money with your adult experiences with money. Can you see any parallels? Can you see any repeating patterns?

3. Jot down in a journal or discuss with a friend or a group any insights you have gained from doing this exercise.

Action Steps

1. List all the times when money was coming into your life easily and all the times when it was not. Note the periods when your financial situation was difficult or you felt as though you were living in a condition of scarcity. Write down points when you felt a sense of abundance in life. What was the sequence of events? What was going on in your life at the time? How were you feeling? Journal about it and contemplate whether there might be any thematic threads coming up around this topic for you.

2. Be curious. Start collecting stories, because you can learn a lot from others. Ask the people you know about their history with money, from their childhood until now. Ask them what they feel their parents taught them to believe about money. Try to collect stories from as wide a range of people as possible, with different backgrounds and from different generations. (Hint: If you can ask your own parents these questions, the answers are often very revealing.)

3. If you meet someone whom you feel has an aspect of their life arranged in a way that you think is desirable, ask them about it. Maybe they have wealth or all the free time they want, or maybe they do what they love. How did they get there? What were the key steps for them? What, if anything, would they do differently if they had it to do over?

CHAPTER TWO

Our Belief Framework
"I'll Believe It When I See It"

We often hear people say "I'll believe it when I see it," but in fact the mechanism works more like "I'll *see* it when I *believe* it," or "I'll believe it; *then* I'll see it."

We see what we believe, quite literally.

Every second of every day, our five senses are bombarded with millions of pieces of data, including a huge range of auditory information, countless sensations (internal and external), more images than we could ever possibly process, and a constantly changing array of body chemicals registering as tastes and smells—not to mention the sensations, tastes, and smells we process from food and drink, from contact with others, and from the environments we live and work in.

All this information is triggering millions of analytical functions in our brains, creating thoughts, categorizing and labeling feelings, sparking emotions, and producing conscious and unconscious commands to our bodies. It is nonstop processing, 24/7. There's a lot going on!

In order for us to be able to function without sensory overload, we have to have a way to filter the information and decide what's important and what's not. The system we use for that is called the *reticular activating system* or RAS. Everything that comes into the brain gets filtered through our RAS.

The RAS is programmed based on your beliefs about yourself and the world. The system has to have some criteria to filter the information; otherwise your brain would be overloaded, and you wouldn't be able to function properly. The RAS filtering criteria is essentially based on what you already believe to be true, relevant, or important.

In other words, your RAS is constantly filtering the information that you're receiving while looking for reference information to support your existing beliefs. This is the system in your brain that ensures you see what you are looking for. That's a really important function! The problem can be that you see little else.

For a simple example of the RAS in action, think about what happens when you're planning to buy a new car. Say you're thinking about a make or model that you have never owned before. Suddenly you start seeing those cars everywhere you go. You might even conclude that type of car is really popular because you're seeing so many of them on the road. But what has really happened is that your RAS has just stopped filtering them out—that's why you're "seeing" them more often.

Because of the way the RAS operates, once we believe something about a person, place, or scenario, we tend to ignore or dismiss evidence that does not fit with our belief, while we look for and accept evidence that serves to confirm our belief. This principle has been established over and over again in psychological studies in a phenomenon known as *confirmation bias.*

A famous 1993 study conducted by Joseph Koehler revealed confirmation bias in action. Koehler's study found that research reports presented to a group of scientists were more likely to be perceived as high quality when the reports agreed with the scientists' prior beliefs about a topic.[1] Experiments have also repeatedly found that people tend to test hypotheses in a one-sided way. They actually search for evidence consistent with the hypothesis they already believe to be true![2]

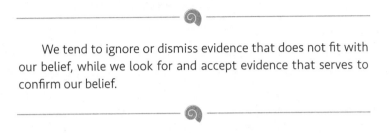

We tend to ignore or dismiss evidence that does not fit with our belief, while we look for and accept evidence that serves to confirm our belief.

The RAS effect can be stronger for emotionally charged issues and for deeply entrenched beliefs. For example, if Sally is set against high-pressure hydraulic mining—known as "fracking"—then she will tend to preferentially seek out information about the negative environmental consequences of this type of mining and discount sources that say it can be done safely. Jeff, on the other hand, is in favor of fracking (or maybe has a financial interest of some sort in it). He will tend to discount reports that warn about the environmental dangers and actively seek evidence to support his view that it is plenty safe.

What Do You Believe?

If we deeply believe something at a subconscious level, then even if we consciously wish things could be different, the power of our subconscious mind ensures that our beliefs get reaffirmed again and again in our everyday experiences. In this way, our subconscious beliefs can actually sabotage our conscious efforts to manifest change.

I'll go through each of the 7 Money Myths one by one as we move through the book. Right now I just want you to consider what effect the wrong kind of programming can have on your experiences. Let me tell you a story to illustrate . . .

When my sister was expecting her first child, she experienced the typical maternal "nesting" instinct. In the late stages of her pregnancy, she cleaned out all the cupboards, stocked up on baby paraphernalia, repainted all the walls in the house, and then decided to replace all the doorknobs on the internal doors. She took the old doorknobs off, but before she got the chance to put the new ones on, the baby came.

He was a gorgeous little boy. And he was a boy who, for the first few years of his life, lived in a house with no doorknobs. So he learned there were two ways to open a door. First, he'd try pushing. If that didn't work, he'd get down on the floor and slide his fingers underneath the door and pull.

One day, my sister and her husband went to look at a new display home. They took their little boy with them. They all walked around, checking out the house. At one point my sister was outside looking at the garden, and she turned to see her little boy through a window.

He'd gone in one of the bedrooms and shut the door behind him by pushing it closed. Then when he wanted to get out of the room, he'd tried his usual trick of sliding his fingers under the door and pulling. Only this house had doorknobs, and that meant the door had clicked shut when it closed. He pulled and pulled and pulled some more. But of course the door would not open. He didn't even know what a doorknob was, so it never occurred to him to use that to open the door.

He must have persisted for a good while pulling the door from underneath, but finally, when his door-opening strategy was clearly not working despite his repeated efforts, he got frustrated and burst into tears. Luckily this was about the time that my sister saw what was happening and was able to come to the rescue.

Like my sister's little boy, if we did not receive the right programming about how to open the door to wealth when we were young, then chances are that the strategies we're using to try to open that door are not going to work for us now. As any good computer programmer will tell you, one of the central tenets of programming is "Rubbish in, rubbish out." Although you may say to yourself on a conscious level that you would like things to be different in your life, if you have the wrong programming, then the innermost workings of your mind will not allow the desired outer change to happen. And that's frustrating!

That's why it's so important for you to read this book—because if any of the 7 Money Myths have made their way into your subconscious mind (and it's very likely that at least some of them have), then they will thwart your efforts to achieve the lasting wealth and financial freedom that you desire.

The *great* news is that you can overwrite your limiting beliefs to bring more wealth and abundance into your life quickly and easily. There are relatively simple ways to reprogram your mind, and I am going to talk about *how* later in the book. But unless you take the reins and actively decide what you want to believe, you will likely remain stuck in your inherited conditioning.

A lot of people focus heavily on the intellect, and neglect the powerful role played by beliefs. That's a mistake I made myself for a long time.

Knowledge Alone Is Not Enough

I have shared with you my own personal story of wealth and success, and how I came to realize that my limiting subconscious beliefs were sabotaging me and blocking me from the attainment of my conscious desires in life. I've also seen subconscious sabotage play out as a big factor in my professional life, having observed it not only in myself, but also in many of the people I've worked with and in the lives of hundreds of clients whom I've coached.

As you know, I'm an economist by trade and a statistician with more than 25 years of professional experience. And as I described, I've worked for the past dozen or so years in the financial-education industry, and for more than a decade before that I was a global financial markets analyst and economic and statistical researcher conducting research for the Reserve Bank of Australia, Nomura Securities in Japan, and one of Australia's largest investment banks. I have an honors degree in economics and econometrics and a master's degree in finance and business administration.

Over the course of my career I've interacted with a lot of people who also have a great deal of knowledge about investing and wealth creation. These individuals spent most of their adult lives devouring as much information as they could on how to create wealth, learning why money flows around the world the way it does. And many of them devoured this knowledge because they had a burning desire for financial freedom.

Yet oddly enough, I saw that some of these same people appeared to be blocked in achieving their goal despite having all the apparent ingredients for success. Some people, I observed, seemed to consistently fail to succeed—even when they really wanted to succeed, and even when the level of knowledge they had attained about how to succeed was of a high standard.

Don't get me wrong. I've also seen plenty of people who've had no problems successfully implementing their knowledge and growing their wealth. But what confused me was the fact that the successful people were not necessarily the cleverest or most knowledgeable of the bunch. Nor were they always the ones most driven to succeed. This really perplexed me.

Even before I had my own epiphany in 2008, I had begun to get the sense that it wasn't necessarily just about knowledge. It wasn't necessarily just about desire either, or effort. So what was the key ingredient? Why did some people succeed while others didn't?

I started to listen very closely to the ways that people spoke about money. And I began to see a connection between the kinds of things that people say—the subtle clues they let slip about their underlying beliefs about money and success—and their actual level of financial success. I slowly connected the dots and realized that the mysterious secret ingredient might just be beliefs.

The Formula

Desire + Knowledge + Belief = Success!

but

Desire + Knowledge – Belief = Frustration!

Suffice it to say that after many years of study and reflection, after the personal epiphany I had about the importance of my own subconscious beliefs, and after much observation and interaction with my clients, I finally got clear on what I felt was the essential formula for success. *And* I understood why some people consistently fail to achieve it.

It's actually a pretty simple formula when you break it down:

Desire + Knowledge + Belief = Success!

but

Desire + Knowledge – Belief = Frustration!

I'm getting ahead of myself though. Let me backtrack a little bit and tell you how I reached this conclusion.

The Wrong Set of Beliefs Leads to Endless Frustration

As you know, I co-own a group of companies called the Trading Pursuits Group, and I currently run those companies as the managing director. My business partner, Daniel Kertcher, is a very smart guy and an excellent educator on financial-market trading with more than 20 years of investing experience.

In our business, we conduct live training courses that teach everyday people how to invest in and trade the financial markets, we provide financial-market analysis services, and we facilitate quick and easy online investing for our clients. As I write this in 2015, we have eight-figure revenues and a team of about 30 staff, and we've been running the business for 14 years. We love teaching people how to become better investors, because Daniel and I are both keen investors ourselves. Practice what you preach, right?

When we were just starting out in our business in 2001 and 2002, the entire operation was just Daniel, his sister, and me. Daniel delivered the training, his sister managed the live training events, and I did the post-event customer support. It was my job to help clients with any questions they might have after they'd completed a training course. I would provide guidance if they were having trouble implementing the strategies or techniques we'd taught them.

Let me say up front that trading the financial markets is not easy, and there is no "magic bullet" method that is always going to work in all market conditions. But we provide a solid education in trading and investing that, if implemented properly, significantly boosts a client's chances of success.

Many of our clients have been incredibly successful implementing the techniques we've taught them. But there was always a percentage that just *could not* make it work. I used to spend a lot of my time trying to help these clients and trying to understand where they were going wrong.

I knew they'd received the same knowledge as everyone else we'd trained. I knew they were trading in exactly the same market conditions as our other clients—those who *were* making it work. And I observed that they had a similar desire for financial success and were actually putting in the required effort. But for some strange reason they were getting a frustratingly different outcome: failure rather than success.

For years, I focused on helping these frustrated clients track back to the one thing that caused them to go wrong. That "thing" was usually easy to find: Maybe they did not put the appropriate risk-management measures in place; maybe they misread an entry or exit signal; maybe they didn't follow their trading plan; maybe they hung on too long to their losing trades; or maybe they even hung on too long to their winning trades, only to watch the market turn around and take back all their previous gains.

There were always reasons that we could identify after the fact. Hindsight is great, isn't it? It's relatively easy to identify *what* the mistake is, or was, after it's happened. What's harder to identify is *why* it happened.

Answering the *why* question turned out to be the key to understanding the behavior and stopping it from becoming an ongoing pattern. In order to do that, I had to ask some questions: What was driving the behavior that led to the wrong choice? What emotions influenced that behavior?

For many people it was just a case of the training not having quite sunk in. They needed some more trading experience. They had to allow themselves to make some mistakes, but to limit the size of those mistakes, before the lessons would really hit home. In other words, the learning for them was in the doing.

But for others, the pattern of messing things up was persistent, and market-trading experience didn't seem to make it go away. Some clients didn't always mess up in the same way, but they just seemed determined to deviate again and again from the trading principles we had taught them. That is, sometimes the common denominator was not *how* they deviated from the rules, but simply the fact that they *would* deviate from them.

I began to suspect that for these clients there was some kind of internal short-circuit going on. These were people who had all the knowledge they needed to succeed, as well as a burning desire to do so, but who weren't succeeding because time and again they did things that undermined the outcome. They would not always do the *same* thing to sabotage their success, but they would always do *something* to sabotage it.

What was causing this strange behavior? On the surface they seemed to want to succeed . . . but maybe underneath, they really didn't.

Case Study: James

I'll give you a typical example. Let's say I had a client called James who asked me for trading support. The very first thing I would do is have him show me the past trades he'd done and to tell me exactly what had happened.

Let's say James got into a trade with a strong view about which direction the thing he was trading was going to move, and maybe even a good rational reason for that, and he really believed the trade was going to be profitable. So he put the trade on and was confident that the value of his investment would go up. But it didn't go up. It went down. However, instead of closing the trade out quickly and cutting his loss, James held on.

James believed that his original reasoning, or perhaps even just his "gut feeling," was right and that the thing would eventually turn around. He didn't want to close the trade because that would crystallize a loss, which would see him miss out on the rebound that he was *sure* would eventually come.

But the investment didn't rebound; it continued to go down, and soon James's account was down even more. So to cover his (now even bigger) loss, he sold down some holdings of another investment he had in his portfolio that had actually been doing well and was in profit. He decided to use some of those profits to cover the losses of the trade he had the strong gut feeling about, but which wasn't doing so well.

James got a psychological payoff for doing that. Selling the winner and taking some of his profits affirmed that he'd been right about that trade, and that made him feel good. Not selling the loser allowed James to avoid admitting that he was wrong about that one, and it meant he could put off having to feel bad about it. He could preserve his hope about eventually being right about that trade. It could still come good . . . right?

Maybe . . . but he'd just committed a portfolio-management sin. What had happened to James's portfolio? He now had relatively less of a winning investment and more of a losing one!

Pure probability (based on existing trends) indicates the winner will probably go on to win some more, and the loser will probably go on to lose some more. If that happened, then not only would James be down even *more* on the loser, but he also wouldn't make as much as he could have if he hadn't sold down the winner to cover the loser. He would end up losing out twice!

It doesn't make sense to behave this way, but you might be surprised to know that many traders do exactly what I've described. Their subconscious need to be right and their fear of being wrong—perhaps driven by some internal judgment that being wrong equates to being "bad" or feeling bad—sabotages their ability to think rationally and results in behavior that undermines their success.

Creating Our Reality

Another example of sabotaging behavior can occur when someone is habituated to having drama in their lives because their inner belief is that turmoil is "normal." Maybe they grew up in a home where their parents fought a lot, drank too much, or were emotionally immature.

Then when they're adults, whenever things are going peacefully and well in their lives, they suddenly find a way to insert some drama to bring things back into their experiential range of what normal is. They might get a little tipsy, decide to drive home, and then get caught drunk driving. Perhaps they suddenly feel cranky for no apparent reason and pick a fight with their partner. Or they might have an accident, tripping and breaking their arm. All of this could be so that their outer experience of life—of having lots of drama—matches their inner belief that drama is normal.

I can relate to this. I've never been drunk driving, but I sure have created my fair share of drama in the past. And I've tended to choose to be in relationships with people who were pretty good at that, too. So I've certainly been guilty of this kind of self-sabotage. I also experienced self-sabotage when it came to money.

As you know, I've experienced my own humbling mistakes regarding wealth. I've made some great money in business and in my investments. I've also made plenty of stupid investment decisions over the years, going into things for the wrong reasons, which then turned out badly. I think this was my experience simply because I believed that kind of crazy, stressful roller-coaster ride was normal.

Over the years I've had to learn that life does not have to be jam-packed with drama all the time. My emotional and financial life can be smooth. It can all be peaceful and easy. Now I have installed a belief that my financial situation is stable and my wealth is steadily growing. And so it is.

Subconscious Sabotage

How can you tell if you're being sabotaged by your subconscious beliefs about money? Well, if your goal is to have more wealth and financial freedom, and you've tried all kinds of ways to achieve your goal but still have not succeeded, then that's a pretty good sign you don't really believe in it.

Frustration with respect to financial freedom is a key indicator of the need to change your mind-set and look at your ingrained money beliefs. A good place to start is by not underestimating the power of the subconscious mind. The subconscious is a tricky beast. Even the process of trying to look at your beliefs can suffer from the effects of subconscious sabotage!

Sabotage by the subconscious mind can manifest in various ways. It might even be manifesting right now . . .

- You may find yourself dismissing evidence that supports an alternative viewpoint to your underlying beliefs.

- You may find yourself in an unreceptive frame of mind toward questioning or changing an underlying belief. For example, you may tell yourself that it is all "too hard" or that you are "too old to change."

- You may have resistance based on your sense of identity or worthiness. For example, you may not want to accept a belief that money can come easily if you've already worked hard to earn what you've got. You may not want to accept it because it could make you feel as if all your effort so far has been futile or is somehow diminished in value. Or you simply may not believe that you deserve things that come to you easily.

- You may tell yourself that you have to do A, B, or C before you can have your conscious desire, but that you don't have time to do A, B, or C—that you are too busy right now. This way you put off the belief conflict indefinitely.

- You may experience a sense of fatigue or an inability to concentrate as you try to gain knowledge that supports a conscious desire but conflicts with an underlying belief. This fatigue is often a physical indication that you have resistance from a subconscious belief.

- If you do make the leap and do make efforts to bring about your conscious desire, you may give up at the first pothole along the road if the conscious desire does not match your subconscious belief. When you get disheartened or give up easily, this may indicate you never really believed the goal was truly possible.

This last point, in my experience with clients, is particularly common. The road to financial freedom is not necessarily a smooth one. Even if you don't have conflicting beliefs, there will be learning experiences along the way. If you *do* have conflicting beliefs, you will be more easily put off by the first setback rather than viewing it as a learning experience. You will be easily discouraged, and you will give up, because giving up will reaffirm your underlying belief that it was never going to work in the first place.

Yes, there will always be some way you can justify why it didn't work. And yes, there will always be plenty of people (who didn't believe in it either) who will agree with you.

How can you overcome this? The things that you are doing to sabotage yourself are *subconscious* . . . that means below the level of your conscious awareness by definition! How can you fight something that you're not even entirely aware of?

Well, you can work on becoming aware of it. There are symptoms—like frustration, like not getting the outcomes you desire despite your best efforts—that can point to the presence of subconscious sabotage in your life. And when you realize that you may have a subconscious block, *Don't fight it,* I say. *Overwrite it.*

It's not always easy, but it is relatively simple to do this—when you know how. I say this because there is a simple formula you can follow (stay tuned!). It's not always easy, because you have to be willing to do the inner work and follow the formula. And sometimes it takes going through a bunch of frustration before you get to that place of willingness.

First, I just want you to start noticing. Reflect on situations past and present, and try to notice patterns in your own behavior with respect to money. Journaling can help with this part; the next seven chapters will be instrumental, too. I will help you identify some of the beliefs that are probably holding you back (the 7 Money Myths), we will work to weaken them together, and then you can choose a set of new beliefs that will support the achievement of your conscious goals and desires. Once you have done that, then you can take some simple steps to program those new beliefs into your subconscious mind.

This process is how you will be able to activate your very own *Abundance Code.*

Beliefs Are Powerful Things

If you have even one of the 7 Money Myths running around in the background of your subconscious mind, then you will likely be blocked at every turn from achieving lasting financial freedom. You will not be able to install your own *Abundance Code.* You will be frustrated.

Even if you acquire a high level of knowledge about how to attain financial freedom, you'll fall down when it comes to implementation. Or even if you achieve some short-term success or financial gain, you'll find it hard to keep. You will, quite literally, sabotage yourself unless you remove these limiting belief programs from your subconscious mind and replace them with beliefs that support your goals.

But please don't feel bad. You're not alone in this. We've all taken on beliefs unconsciously as a part of our upbringing. That's normal, and it's even as it should be. We needed to take on a belief framework when we were young in order to help us make sense of the world, to protect ourselves and be safe, and to avoid overloading our growing brains with too much information.

We had to learn some essential survival facts early on from our parents, like the notion that stoves are hot and can burn us, so we shouldn't touch them, or the idea that it can be dangerous to talk to strangers, so we should avoid doing that. Beliefs act as shortcut protection measures when we're young, because we actually don't have the proper discrimination needed to protect ourselves without them.

Later on in life, we can hopefully modify or relax the beliefs to allow for more freedom in opportunities and outcomes. For example, we learn that stoves are not always hot. They're only hot when they're turned on, so it's okay to touch them when they aren't, for example, if we want to wipe them clean. We figure out that it's okay to talk to strangers sometimes because they're not always dangerous, and because it's actually hard to make new friends or find a mate if we never talk to anyone new. If we didn't modify and relax those beliefs, we would be stuck with a really dirty stovetop and very few friends.

This is the kind of thing that happens when we haven't modified or relaxed key beliefs that we may have previously taken on for good reasons at the time. We find ourselves frustrated and constrained in life. When we feel that way, it's just because we have a belief that no longer suits us since it's too restrictive. When we want more from life than our beliefs will let us experience, that's when frustration happens.

Sometimes, even after we've grown up and could handle more relaxed beliefs that allow for more opportunities and freedom, our programs have still not caught up. They are stuck on their original setting, even if that's no longer appropriate.

So few people actually take the time to consider the power that some of the belief programs we unwittingly took on when we were little—and may not have subsequently modified—can have in limiting the outcomes we experience in our lives as adults.

Our subconscious beliefs determine the conscious reality that we experience.

That's a powerful statement. And it's vital that you understand, so I'll say it again: *Our subconscious beliefs determine the conscious reality that we experience.*

Why? Remember the reticular activating system and confirmation bias, as well as the evidence I've collected over years of working with all kinds of individuals to reach their financial goals? What you are aware of is what you see and experience in the world around you. Your beliefs will cause you to gather evidence and support to maintain what you already believe to be true. And this will lead you to experience one of these two key equations:

Desire + Knowledge + Belief = Success

but

Desire + Knowledge – Belief = Frustration

The equations are so simple, and yet so important to understand. They are a core insight. Let's put it another way:

- Having the "know-how" is very important—that's true—but it's equally important to make sure that you have the right belief structure to support that knowledge.

  No matter how many techniques you learn for creating wealth, no matter how many tricks of the trade you have, and no matter how clever your plan is, if you do not have a belief system that supports your goal, then you will *not* be able to achieve it. Period.

  Knowledge is important, but knowledge alone is not enough.

- When your conscious desires do not fully align with your subconscious beliefs, the outcome is *frustration* rather than success. If you have limiting beliefs on board, you need to identify them and change them if you want to succeed.

For example, if you believe that you can't manage money well, then you won't manage money well—even if you are taught how to do so. If you believe that "you have to work hard for your money," then you will find that you have to work hard for everything you get. If you believe in the concept of "easy come, easy go," then you'll find that you can't hang on to money that comes to you easily.

- You will only truly accept into your life that which matches your underlying belief structure.

In other words, no matter how much you want something on a conscious level, if you do not believe it is possible on a subconscious level, then you will simply find that you are *unable* to bring your conscious desire to fruition. You will sabotage yourself at every turn so that your outward experience of life does not contradict your most deeply held inner beliefs.

Choose What You Believe

When you think about what you want, do you come up with a whole host of reasons that justify why you don't have it or why you can't have it—reasons that arise from your inherent doubts about being able to attain your desires?

The truth of *why you don't have it* actually lies in your sub-conscious beliefs. Why don't you have the life you want? Simply because you don't believe it's possible. Still, that's not going to stop you from justifying the situation to yourself.

If you're not already living the reality you desire, then, whether you're aware of it or not, you have definitely justified *why not* to yourself in myriad ways. There are lots of justifications that may seem perfectly reasonable to you about why you don't have the lifestyle you want.

For example, maybe you push attaining your desires off into the future by saying that you need to do A, B, or C first. Perhaps you think you've been unlucky or lacked the opportunities so far to have the life you want. Or it could be that you tell yourself you've had to make sacrifices to balance what you want against what you or your family needs. All of this may sound very reasonable. It makes sense to you because it fits with what you believe.

But what if what you believe is not necessarily true? What if it's not even helpful—that is, what if it doesn't actually help you to get what you want in life?

The belief structures that many of us carry encompass a set of rules for getting ahead in life. A lot of us follow these rules unquestioningly. Here are some common ones:

- Study hard at school.

- Graduate with qualifications that will be desirable to employers.

- Get a "good" job even if you don't like it.

- Accept that you have to make sacrifices (family, leisure time, health, youth, and vitality) in order to get ahead.

- Keep your head down, work hard, and don't complain.

- Let the corporate world dictate what you are worth.

- *Always* play by the rules.

Does it have to be this way? No!

There *is* another reality you can access. You don't necessarily have to work hard for every penny you get. You don't have to work nine to five (or worse). You can do what you love. You can determine your own worth. You can remain authentic and true to yourself and still get ahead. You can define for yourself what "getting ahead" means. You can be financially free. You can have it all.

Yes! You can!

Do you believe it?

This is not a trivial question, so let me ask you again: *Do you believe it?*

This is the key: The thing that most people don't understand is that you can't access this reality merely by wanting it; you also have to believe it. If you truly want to change your manifest experience—to gain more financial freedom and an easier path to wealth than having to work hard for every penny you earn—you must dismantle your subconscious blockages to attaining financial freedom and replace them with beliefs that support what you really want in life.

When you have achieved a subconscious reprogramming that aligns your subconscious beliefs with your conscious desires—and you combine this with the appropriate knowledge—just watch how rapidly your reality shifts! It does not take long before you *see* what you *believe*.

Case Study: A Dream Job

Back when I was working at a major Australian investment bank in their funds-management area, the main thing I wanted to be doing for them was econometric modeling. That's a very specialized field that's essentially the intersection of statistical analysis and economics. It's my specialty. I studied it for many years at university, and it's the thing that I was really good at.

There are very few jobs in that rarified field, and for some reason I decided to believe that I wouldn't be able to get a job just doing econometrics. I believed that I would also have to do some economic analysis, too, even though that wasn't what I really loved to do, nor was it what I was super talented at doing. I mean, I was a competent economist, but I was an excellent econometrician.

Sure enough, when I got the job at the investment bank, they said they wanted me to do both economic analysis and econometrics. I accepted the job because I'd already told myself I'd never get a job just doing econometrics.

Then as things unfolded, there turned out to be a lot more economic analysis than econometrics. Over the years, the imbalance between what I really wanted to do and what I got to do in that job just became worse and worse.

One day I reached a breaking point. I got very clear on what I wanted, and it was not spending my days on economic analysis. I decided that I'd start looking for a job where I could do econometrics full time. I saw myself doing that, and I committed internally to the idea that it really was possible to get a position where I could have exactly what I wanted.

Literally three days later, my bosses called me in for a chat. I clearly remember thinking, *Uh-oh.* Then I thought, *Wow, they know. I'm not living up to my potential here, and they probably think I'm not trying hard enough.* I felt so disappointed in myself that I assumed they must be disappointed in me, too. So I thought they were going to fire me.

Instead, they said, "Julie, we've decided that we really need to beef up our econometric models. Can you start working on that for us full time? We'll assign someone else to your economic analysis duties right away."

Wow. You could have tipped me over with a feather!

Now, was it a coincidence that as soon as I changed my belief about what was possible in my life and internally committed myself to it that my external reality shifted as well?

Lose the Judgments

Most of us have grown up taking on beliefs about money that aren't necessarily helpful to us or true. We've received a whole bunch of loaded messages about what money means from our parents, our friends, and society in general, when in truth, money is just the physical manifestation of an idea.

That's right, money is just an *idea* . . . an idea written on a piece of paper. Sometimes it doesn't even make it onto paper! Sometimes it's just numbers in a computer—numbers created by the banking system. It's true: All that stuff in your wallet is just an idea. All those numbers in your bank account—just an idea. The income you get from your job, your business, or your investments—just an idea.

If we have applied one idea for a product, service, deal, trade, or whatever, and turned it into another idea—money, or numbers on a bank statement—well, there's nothing inherently wrong with that, is there? No!

Sure, there are ethical principles that are still important to follow. I don't encourage you to lie, cheat, or steal. But if there's an easy way to make money, and you understand it, is it okay to use it? Of course it's okay! If there's a path to getting ahead in life that doesn't involve endless long hours of work, is it okay to take it? Of course it's okay! Go for it!

Let's consider some new territory for our beliefs about money:

- Let's lose the idea that there is not enough to go around and instead embrace the idea of limitless abundance.

- Let's shed our old belief that we have to work hard for our money and instead make a bold step into a future where money can come easily to us.

- Let's free ourselves from the idea that we have to do something to "deserve" having money. Let's realize and truly believe that it's okay for us to have money now, that we deserve financial freedom—everyone does—and that we don't have to do any sort of penance to justify it.

- Let's liberate ourselves from the suspicion that having money will somehow corrupt us or make us evil.

- Let's clear from our minds all obstacles to manifesting financial freedom in our lives.

It may be difficult for you to believe all of this right now, but I assure you it will feel a lot more attainable and possible by the end of this book. It's a paradigm shift, and that shift will start to happen on a subtle, subconscious level as you proceed through each chapter.

We've all inherited values and beliefs from our parents, our role models, and our social and cultural upbringing. There was no avoiding that, and many of those values and beliefs were intended to protect us. So if it just so happens that some of your beliefs aren't helping you to achieve your goals in life, understand that it's not your fault, and it's not really anyone else's fault either.

Now that you are all grown up, though, it's time to examine the values and beliefs you have taken on—about work and money, about your "deservingness" and worth, amongst other things. It's time to decide: Do these beliefs really serve you? Or are they holding you back subconsciously from achieving your goal of financial freedom?

Shifting Your Beliefs

Through my own personal journey, I've learned many excellent techniques for belief change, and I'm going to share some of those with you in Chapter 10 of this book. Now, resist the urge to just skip forward to that chapter! There is some important psychological groundwork we need to cover first. Just knowing that your beliefs create your reality is not enough; there's a specific dismantling process that needs to happen, and it's best to do this step-by-step.

We'll look at the most commonly held beliefs about money and wealth that hold many people back from achieving financial freedom—the 7 Money Myths. I'll go through each myth one by one over the course of the next seven chapters. The purpose of examining the myths individually is twofold:

1. To help you identify whether you might be holding these or similar beliefs, which may be thwarting your efforts to achieve financial freedom.

2. To introduce an element of *doubt* regarding the validity of these commonly held subconscious beliefs

in order to begin viewing them as *myths* that do not
have to be true for you if you don't want them to be.

If you want to weaken the hold of a limiting belief on your
subconscious, the introduction of doubt around that belief is
an important first step. That statement is backed up by a lot of
research and is a principle that has been used for many years in
cognitive therapy (CT). This type of psychotherapy was developed
in the late 1960s by an American psychiatrist named Aaron T.
Beck. According to Beck's model, many psychological disorders
can be traced back to "errors" in thinking (or cognition), which
are the result of dysfunctional beliefs. Beck argued that it is important for these cognitive errors to be recognized and acknowledged
by the patient, with the assistance of the therapist, so that effective progress can be made in treatment.

Throughout the rest of the book, we will take an in-depth
look at our most commonly held beliefs about money, and we
will question their validity. Where appropriate, I will provide case
studies and cite research in order to help you examine critically—
and hopefully introduce an element of doubt around—beliefs that
you may not have previously thought much about. This will help
you to weaken the hold of those beliefs on your mind.

Introducing doubt about the validity of limiting beliefs is
really important. But that alone probably won't do the full job.
You'll also need to overwrite the limiting beliefs with new ones
that will allow for more freedom and abundance in your life. And
you may also need to address your daily habits in order to help
support and cement that underlying belief-change process.

Adding therapy around habitual behaviors into the cognitive
therapy mix began to be embraced by psychotherapists in the 1970s
and prompted the evolution of a broader range of psychotherapeutic techniques, which are now referred to collectively as cognitive
behavior therapy (CBT). This is a very successful and widely used
psychotherapy protocol, the efficacy of which has been verified
by numerous scientific studies. In fact, CBT is probably the most
highly tested and verified psychotherapeutic approach of all.

This book is not about CBT, and I am not a CBT practitioner—let me be clear about that. However, throughout the following chapters, I will guide you through an approach that has a lot of synergies with modern CBT and that employs many strategies and methods to engage the subconscious mind in achieving meaningful belief change so that you can create an abundant life now.

Try to take the chapters in sequence. It's actually *not* the kind of work where I would encourage you to skip around, dip in and out, or skim over parts. This process will work best if you take the chapters in the order they are presented.

If you're seeking to create a new reality, a great place to start is by weakening the foundations that the old reality rests upon. So we're going to begin by exposing the old belief system and acknowledge how and why it does not actually serve your goals. I want you to see that these old programs are just someone else's stories—*myths* that do not have to be true for you anymore.

That's why we're going to examine each of the 7 Money Myths one by one. Let's start in the next chapter by looking at the number one most commonly believed myth about money—the myth of *scarcity*.

Digging Deep

1. What rules about getting ahead in life did you learn when you were growing up? Were you taught that studying or learning a trade and then getting a job and working hard was the best path to success?

2. How have those rules affected the path you took in life?

3. What do you think about the statement that money is just an idea? How do you see that playing out in your life?

Action Steps

1. What are your strongest desires in life? Write them out, without any judgment about whether you currently believe you could have those things or not. A great way to get to this information is to ask yourself, *If money were not an obstacle, what would I be doing? Where would I be living? How would my life be different?*

    First, just make the list without editing yourself or listening to any internal voice that might be saying, *But you can't have that because of A, B, and C reasons.*

2. Now, take each item on your list and start to write out all the objections to it that your internal voice was putting forward. Why do you think you might not be able to have those things you desire? List the reasons. Don't just dismiss your internal objections; take the time to write them down and acknowledge their existence.

3. Start forming a mental picture of your ideal life. Based on the answers to the questions already posed: If money were not an obstacle, what would your ideal life look like? I mean envision the actual mental pictures. Where would you be? What would you be doing? Who would you be with? Would you be smiling?

4. Keep an eye out for images that resonate with your concept of your ideal life. If you see a picture you like in a magazine, one that feels like it represents part of your ideal life, then clip it out and put it in a file. Call it your "ideal life" file. This will come in handy later, when we talk about vision boards in Chapter 10.

CHAPTER THREE

Money Myth #1: Scarcity
"Money Doesn't Grow on Trees"

For most of us born into the working and middle classes, "Money doesn't grow on trees" is a well-worn saying. When someone makes this statement, they are affirming a belief in scarcity.

Yes, it is true in a literal sense that money doesn't grow on trees in the way that flowers or fruit do. However, often it's made of trees! I'm talking about paper money, cash, numbers printed on pieces of paper that we collectively agree to designate as having value as a medium of exchange.

Mostly, though, the saying is a metaphor. Parents use it to urge their children to value what they have and not complain, because it was hard-won and they are lucky to have it. The statement has been used as a way of explaining that we can't always get what we want because of some notion that there really isn't enough to go around. In other words, there isn't that much of this stuff called money, so you'd better watch how much you spend. This is a Scarcity Mind-Set, not an Abundance Mind-Set.

The Scarcity Mind-Set is also reflected in sayings like "Waste not, want not," and "Watch your pennies, and the dollars will look after themselves."

This way of thinking is based on the idea that everyone has to compete to grab his or her share of the pie. There is also a belief that the pie is too small to feed everyone adequately, so someone always has to miss out. Some people even believe the pie is shrinking! This mind-set gives rise to the idea that hoarding is the way to go and generosity is pretty dangerous, because the next time you turn around there could be nothing left.

Beliefs about scarcity are rooted in the experiences of past generations who lived through revolutions, wars, famines, and the Great Depression—times when money and food were hard for people to come by. These beliefs have been conveyed through the use of common sayings and have resulted in subtle subconscious programming.

Our ancestors unwittingly passed scarcity beliefs down to us. They weren't trying to be mean; they were trying to protect us. If there really *isn't* enough to go around, then those beliefs might be helpful protection mechanisms, causing us to be very careful and ration out whatever we've got so that it can last as long as possible.

But there's been a huge amount of progress in the last 100 years. Could it be that scarcity is sometimes a result of specific circumstances or primitive or unevolved social and political systems, but *not* a universal truth? Even if a belief in scarcity is something that was once circumstantially valid, does that necessarily mean it's always going to be valid? Pretty much everything about modern life is different to how things once were. Is it correct to assume (as many of us do, on the level of beliefs) that nothing has really changed?

Does Scarcity Stack Up?

Let's consider for a moment the notions of scarcity and abundance. As much as we humans like to think that everything is so limited and that the essentials of life are always in danger of running out, our planet represents a system that is based largely on abundance. For example, the sun keeps on pumping out energy, day in and day out, regardless of what happens here on Earth. The sun is relentless in its abundance. All of the ecosystems on Earth are based around taking advantage of the sun's abundance.

Most of our notions of limited resources link back to perceived limits in the supply of energy. The main ingredient for the rapid growth of the economic and technological system we live in today has been fossil fuel, which is extracted from the ground and burned for energy.

This resource is indeed limited, but the application of human intelligence is not. We humans are now very busy using the power of our minds to overcome the problem of limited fossil fuel. There is a virtually limitless supply of energy available that we can potentially harness from the light of the sun, from the power contained within every atom, from the Earth's geothermal energy, from the power of the wind and water, and even from biofuels (such as decaying vegetable matter and vegetable oils).

Doesn't it stand to reason, with the sun always pumping out a huge supply of energy for our planet, that we actually live within a system of abundance?

Let's look at just one of these power sources. There is currently more than 5,000 times more solar energy falling on the planet's surface than the human race uses in a year.[1] Plants convert the energy of sunlight to feed their cells, providing food and oxygen to feed the animals on our planet, including us.

Our planetary ecosystem is obviously extremely complex, but one of the most basic laws of physics states that energy can never be destroyed; it can only be converted from one form into another. So doesn't it stand to reason, with the sun always pumping out a huge supply of energy for our planet, that we actually live within a system of abundance? As a species, we haven't even begun to fully tap into the power of the sun, so why do we believe in scarcity so resolutely?

The answer may come back to our cognitive biases. We talked before about the confirmation bias driven by the reticular activating system, but we have another powerful cognitive behavior: the *negativity bias*. This is the tendency to give more weight to negative information and experiences than positive information and experiences.

Tigers and Terror: Looking for Danger

In their eye-opening book *Abundance: The Future Is Better Than You Think,* Peter H. Diamandis and Steven Kotler discuss in detail the effect that our cognitive biases have on the way we view the world. Their book is very important to read if you want to weaken the Scarcity Mind-Set. Check it out at www.abundancethebook.com. I have no affiliation in promoting it; I just think it's great. It discusses in a lot more detail some things that I will briefly skim over now, including the negativity bias.

Here's an easy way to understand where our negativity bias has come from: Those amongst our ancestors who assumed that lions only ever wanted to eat them survived better. "Prepare for the worst" is a mind-set that has its advantages in a savage world. It's just that this is not the world we live in today.

Most people in modern times are free from the threat of bloodthirsty predators pouncing on them every time they walk around a corner. Now our negativity bias manifests in our distinct preference for viewing negative news, violent crime shows, and movies with terrible battle scenes. It seems we love to see stories about tragedy, blood, and conflict played out every night on our TV screens. It's almost as if our brains need to see stories with themes that resonate with the primal battle for survival—perhaps so that we can feel more alive—and maybe that's just the way we are wired.

Think about it. We evolved as a species in harsh circumstances. Before the advent of agriculture, when we foraged and hunted for all of our food and had limited ways to store it, survival was an everyday struggle. If the weather turned bad, we might die. If we encountered predators, we might die. If we cut ourselves and the wound got infected, we might die. If all other conditions were perfect but we didn't find enough food or water, we might die. We probably felt very alive every single day that we survived, because we might easily not have made it. There was a thinner line between life and death.

In the developed world today, we have overcome many of our basic survival obstacles. We don't need to hunt. Instead, our food is delivered to stores where we can swap it for this funny paper that has some numbers printed on it or for the swipe of a card so that some numbers get moved around in a database. We are mostly protected from the weather in our safe, cocoon-like houses and offices. And thanks to antibiotics, we rarely die from infections anymore.

Could it be that in an evolutionary sense, from the perspective of a nervous system that has been primed for millennia for a daily life-or-death struggle, that's a little boring? Perhaps we seek adrenaline-pumping activities in sports and recreation (especially when we're young and in our evolutionary prime) to make ourselves feel that sense of being alive, of being on the edge, of being a little closer to death. Could we also seek parallel struggles in our entertainment—representations of the high-stakes battle to have enough, to be strong enough to survive—in order to fill the evolutionary void?

But isn't it all just harmless entertainment? Not really, because that kind of stimulus affects our brains. It affects the way we think and how we see the world. And what it leads to is a view of the world based on conflict, need, and scarcity.

Even if our brains are naturally inclined toward holding scarcity beliefs and our nervous systems are primed to want to consume scary, adrenaline-pumping, threatening, and negative media content, that does not mean that scarcity, fear, and threat are an accurate representation of our reality!

Combating the Negativity Bias

Many years ago when I was a university student, I personally noticed that if I watched the nightly news and made a habit of reading the newspapers, my outlook on the world started to get pretty negative and dark. I even started to think that there was little hope for humanity, to suspect that we would inevitably screw up on some grand scale and that millions upon millions would die. I developed intense fears about things like global disease pandemics, world wars, nuclear holocausts, overpopulation, pollution, global warming, water shortages, famines, and natural disasters . . . not to mention closer-to-home fears about violence, urban isolation, and the consequences of the dissolution of community.

The interesting thing is that all of these negative outcomes are *possible,* and they certainly are scary, but they are not as *likely* as we are led to believe. And that's because our media coverage is so skewed toward the negative.

I found the list of things to be afraid of was endless, and I began to feel increasingly hopeless about the future. It was making me depressed. So I decided to do a "negative news" detox. I stopped reading the newspapers and watching the news on TV.

I didn't want to be totally uninformed, so if I heard about something going on in the world that I wanted to know more about, I researched it for myself. I used the skills I had honed working as an economic and statistical researcher to seek out reliable sources of information (looking for facts rather than someone else's opinion), and I tried to form my own opinions on the matter rather than letting myself be fed whatever spin the media had decided to put on it.

I also actively sought out sources of information about exciting new developments that could positively impact the future. I subscribed to a range of magazines like *New Scientist, Discover,* and *Scientific American.* What I learned was that technological innovation was—and is—providing an amazing amount of hope for our world. In the pages of these science magazines were stories about innovative solutions to lots of seemingly insurmountable global problems relating to disease, hunger, water, and energy shortages.

By detoxing from negative news that focused on problems, sensationalism, and negative spin, and by doing my own research and reading publications that talked about solutions, my whole outlook and mind-set soon began to shift. I started to become hopeful about the world again.

That was more than 20 years ago. I am still very careful to keep the amount of "news" I watch to the bare minimum required for my work (so that I can stay on top of developments in financial markets). These days I still love reading science magazines, watching inspiring videos about progress and innovation, and listening to podcasts from great minds that are taking a solution-oriented approach.[2]

It's amazing how much this simple shift freed up my mind-set. It helped weaken my belief in scarcity, because I was able to disconnect from my own inherent negativity bias. I started to see that things were not quite so dire after all. My eyes were opened to all the positive things that were happening in the realms of science and technology that were actually making the world a better place to live.

Sure, there were still plenty of problems left to solve, but I began to see that solutions were possible. That helped me to feel better about the future and to believe that even more abundance might be just around the corner, instead of fearing the end of life as we know it.

A naysayer might declare that all I achieved through this shift was to put on a pair of rose-colored glasses. Well, that's possible, yes . . . but I don't think that's the full story.

Perceiving the Truth

We *can* start to change the reality we see by changing the way in which we stimulate our brain. Our brain's wiring actually shifts depending on how we use it. This is known as *neuroplasticity.* So the way in which we choose to nourish and build our brain has an impact on the way we think.

This is where not only beliefs but also habits—such as whether or not we choose to watch the news every night—can play an important role if we want to change the way we see things. And maybe that is exactly what putting on rose-colored glasses means. If we choose to, we can change the lens through which we view the world.

But if our perception is so malleable, then what is real? As a statistician by trade, I'm inclined to say that numbers are real. Of course, you can always torture the data and get it to confess if you are hell-bent on proving a particular viewpoint, but good statisticians don't do that. They let the numbers tell the story. And the data, if you look at it, backs me up. Things are not that bad.

Diamandis and Kotler, in their abundance book, cite the work of Hans Rosling, an academic who analyzes data from countries all around the world and puts that data into a visual format that makes it easy to see what's going on in terms of global trends.[3] Rosling compellingly argues that not only have we made extraordinary progress in improving global living standards in the last half century (especially, contrary to popular belief, for those in the poorest countries), but that if we continue on this path, the future could be even better.[4]

Even though conflicts from around the globe are reported nightly on the news, we're actually living in one of the most peaceful periods ever by historical standards. That's according to Dr. Steven Pinker, an acclaimed author and Harvard psychology professor. Conflicts in the current age are often broadcast for all to see, creating the perception that violence is on the rise. But that's not really true. We're just seeing it more. There are actually fewer conflicts today, and wars don't kill as many people as they did, for example, in the Middle Ages. The world has become more peaceful.

Of course further improvements are both needed and desired! But amazing progress has already been made. Most people just don't realize *how much* progress has been made, and that is because of our predisposition toward negative news due to our cognitive negativity bias.

This is the *real* news: Exciting innovations have already unlocked greater abundance for the world, and more are on the way. As science continues to explore the mysteries of matter and energy, we see that the only limits are those present within our own minds.

Scarcity is not a fact. It is not a trend. As a worldview, it is not even backed up by the data. Scarcity is just a belief that no longer serves us.

We have certainly moved beyond the primitive, caveman, survival-oriented lifestyle. And although we will continue to stride forward, it is helpful to recognize that our cognitive processes, biases, and wiring have not necessarily caught up. It may be our evolutionary tendency to believe in scarcity, but fight that tendency! Recognize that it is largely a cognitive bias, not a fact.

Moving Out of "Scare-City"

Although I will discuss seven different limiting beliefs about money, in a way, *scarcity* is at the core of them all. It's actually a mind-set that underlies, in one manner or another, all limiting beliefs about money. I like to call this worldview "Scare-City" because I think *it's a place where we live in fear.*

The Scarcity Mind-Set tells us to be untrusting in the bounty of the earth, untrusting of others and of ourselves. It drives us to hoard and to compete. It urges us to be envious and perhaps even suspicious of others, to disconnect and protect what we've got, and to grasp whatever we can in the meantime for our own safety. It tells us that some disaster is coming eventually, and we'd better be prepared.

It also tells us that we are not enough just the way we are, but that we have to do something to justify our existence. It tells us to sacrifice what we really love in order to get what we are told we need. It tells us to conform and to play by the rules.

The Scarcity Mind-Set puts us on a never-ending hamster wheel. It keeps us tired and constrained, feeling isolated and alone. It saps our life-force energy.

Compare this with the Abundance Mind-Set. This is relaxed. It tells us there is enough, that *we* are enough, and to follow our joy in all things. It's a mind-set where we view ourselves as part of an ecosystem, where everything is interconnected.

Because it's more like an ecosystem, I like to think of it as the "Abundance Forest." Compared to Scare-City, the Abundance Forest is a place where we are all connected, where the prosperity of each is intrinsically linked to the prosperity of all. It's a place where the individual parts combine like a symphony to create a far greater and more integrated whole . . . yet where every individual is unique and valuable, just the way they are.

In the Abundance Forest, we are encouraged to share and to collaborate. Instead of seeing ourselves in competition battling for our piece of the pie of limited resources, we start to see ourselves as part of a community in which we are all able to grow and thrive together. It's a place where diversity and creativity bear amazing fruits. It is a place where generosity and community spirit are natural consequences of the recognition that we are all interdependent. We do not thrive in isolation.

This mind-set encourages us to connect, to inspire, and to create from our boundless imaginations. While it's okay to prepare ourselves for adverse events, the Abundance Mind-Set reminds us to not become obsessive about that. We are able to remain hopeful and optimistic so that we can spot opportunity when it knocks instead of being preoccupied with fears about risk and disaster scenarios.

When we operate from the Abundance Mind-Set we feel full of purpose, full of energy, and we have a seemingly limitless drive. We engage this drive without striving, grasping, or hoarding. And what comes back to us is abundance, satisfaction, and joy.

How do we make this shift? By overwriting our belief in scarcity and embracing a new paradigm in our lives—the paradigm of abundance.

Parashifting? What's That?

The more open, abundant, sharing, free, and generous we are in our hearts and minds, the more we experience kindheartedness, generosity, connection, freedom, and abundant wealth in the outer world.

Why is that? Well, once we're no longer operating within a system or mind-set of limitation, everything opens up. When we make that paradigm shift, we immediately feel less scared, and we immediately feel more optimistic and hopeful about the future.

That allows us to shift our focus away from our fears about disaster scenarios and to start seeing possibilities. Once we start seeing possibilities around us, then we can start seeing opportunities.

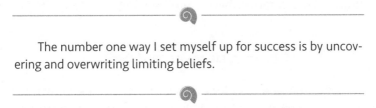

The number one way I set myself up for success is by uncovering and overwriting limiting beliefs.

It's not a big leap from there to start imagining and forming plans about how the new opportunities we're seeing can be used to bring about greater levels of abundance and freedom in our lives. When we are focused on fear, we just don't see as many opportunities. They kind of pass us by. . . . So a lot can change through a simple paradigm shift.

A paradigm shift is something that is just a choice. It can happen right now. I call it *parashifting*. Yes, I made that word up. It encapsulates a lot for me. One of the things that the term *parashifting* expresses for me is that it's not necessarily a "do it and then you're done" kind of change. It could be . . . and I don't want to rule that out for anyone . . . but my experience of it is more like a cycle of forgetting and remembering.

Sometimes I forget to be abundant and slip back into the Scarcity Mind-Set. It's certainly pretty easy for that to happen when it's often the dominant perspective I encounter in society, in the news, and in business.

However, by staying aware of the signs that indicate to me that a slip has occurred—symptoms like frustration, inner negativity, and a lack of flow in my life—and by continuing to clean my mental house in terms of my subconscious programming (more on this in Chapter 10), I gradually attain a more and more solid footing in the Abundance Mind-Set. Also, by choosing to surround myself with other people who are parashifting themselves into the Abundance Mind-Set, I actively choose reinforcement for that paradigm.

That's why I like to think of *parashifting* as a verb—as something that is a process. It's really an evolution for me. Parashifting is about noticing, remembering, and setting myself up for success.

Observe, Uncover, and Refocus

The number one way I set myself up for success is by uncovering and overwriting limiting beliefs. I replace them with positive beliefs that support me in expressing and experiencing abundance in everything I think, say, and do. For example, one belief that played out very strongly in my life in the past was that I could either be wealthy or I could be happy, but not both. When I noticed that pattern surfacing again and again in my life, and when I realized that it pointed to an underlying belief that was not serving me, then it was relatively easy for me to overwrite that belief.

I overwrote it with a belief that I could be happy *and* I could be wealthy. Now, I was careful not to limit myself in my new belief. (I'll talk more about the importance of having well-formed replacement beliefs that are not limiting in Chapter 10.) In this case, I was careful that I did not install the slightly different, but still limiting, belief that I have to be wealthy in order to be happy . . . or that I have to be happy in order to be wealthy.

I was careful to install the belief that I can be wealthy and I can be happy at the same time. I can be wealthy even if I happen to not be overly happy, and I can be happy even if I happen to not be overly wealthy. So in my new belief structure, these states are independent of each other and able to coexist at the same time. Both conditions are possible, and one does not cancel out the other.

The key to this process is to first notice the unhelpful pattern that is surfacing in your life. It's usually a pattern of frustration. Until you notice where frustration and blockage are happening, you may not be able to uncover the beliefs that are driving them.

When I notice a pattern of frustration in my life, I know that I need to look at what beliefs might be the root cause of that pattern. Then I need to design new beliefs to overwrite the old beliefs—new beliefs that will support the fulfillment of my desires in life rather than thwart me and cause frustration. If I still notice unhelpful patterns emerging, then I revisit the beliefs and rework them further.

I'm not perfect—I'm a glorious work in progress! And that's why I try to remember to be gentle with myself if I do slip from time to time back into living in Scare-City. Instead of beating myself up about it, I just resolve to return my focus to living and breathing deeply in the Abundance Forest.

The compassionate and nonjudgmental return to focus is actually a technique that is used a lot in meditation. For example, say you are observing the inflow and outflow of the breath as your focus during a meditation session. You suddenly realize that for the last ten minutes instead of focusing on your breath, you have been thinking about how you forgot to hang out the washing . . . or about what you're going to have for dinner . . . or about the argument you had with your mother, like, five years ago. . . . Well, what do you do?

Hopefully, your meditation teacher will guide you to notice that you have lost focus and simply to return your attention to observing your breath.

Don't judge. Don't dwell. Just return to focus.

Your instructor might also tell you to be easy on yourself because losing focus at times is kind of inevitable. You can't just tell your thoughts to stop. But you can choose to let them pass across your mind and return to focusing on your breath.

Similarly, once I recognize that I have slipped back into living in Scare-City, I gently remind myself that I am parashifting so that I can live each day in the Abundance Forest. I remind myself that parashifting is a choice—a choice that I make over and over again until it becomes a habit. So I return to my focus on abundance. I return to choosing abundance in my thoughts, words, and intentions; and I return to expressing abundance in my actions.

Case Study: Greg

I have a friend named Greg who once experienced in a profound and memorable way the powerful effect that a Scarcity Mind-Set can have.

When Greg was about 13, he really wanted a ten-speed bicycle. And not just any ten-speed bike—he wanted a really good one. The one he wanted was displayed in the window of the local bike shop. It was a beauty. He'd had his eye on it for a while.

So he asked his father if he could have the bike as a gift. He took his dad down to the bike shop to look at it.

"Please, please, please, Dad! I really want it," he begged.

His father replied, "Well, son, I'll tell you what: If you save up half the cost of this bike, then I'll put in the other half of the money and get it for you."

Greg was inspired, and he worked really hard to save up his half of the money for the bike. He mowed lawns and delivered newspapers; he did odd jobs for the neighbors . . . all the stuff that kids sometimes do to earn extra money. As he worked, he kept his mind firmly on his goal. He saw himself having a ball riding that amazing ten-speed bike as soon as he had saved up half the money for it.

Finally he reached his goal of earning half the cost of the bike, and he gave the cash to his dad. He was so excited! He couldn't wait to get his new bike.

When the day came, he bounded out of bed. His dad told him the bike was waiting for him in the garage. He ran down to look, but when he opened the door to the garage his heart fell.

His father had bought him a cheaper bike than the one Greg had pointed out to him in the bike-shop window! Greg couldn't believe it. He felt a crushing disappointment . . . and a deep sense of betrayal.

Even though he had given his dad half the money for the more expensive bike, his dad had bought him something cheaper—meaning his dad had effectively put in less than half of the money. His dad had reneged on the deal.

Why did his father do that? My theory: He couldn't help himself because he was in the grip of the Scarcity Mind-Set!

I'm not sure how Greg's father justified in his own mind what he'd done. I think most people would agree it was a pretty bad example of parenting, and so it would be difficult to come up with a rational-sounding explanation. But in the end, beliefs are not rational. Very likely, the subconscious belief in scarcity just *would not* allow him to follow through on his promise.

Greg's dad had set up what could have been a good opportunity for him to deepen his relationship with his son; but because of his Scarcity Mind-Set, he ended up turning it into a psychologically wounding event. It was something Greg never forgot and never really forgave, and it was an incident that I believe really damaged their relationship.

Furthermore, what might this experience have taught Greg to believe about life? I can't speak for Greg on this, but perhaps he coded this incident to mean that he would get shortchanged in life—that the outcomes of his desires would always be somewhat less than he hoped for. That would not be a very helpful belief for Greg to have, and it would no doubt lead to a lot of frustration. But you can see how he might have installed that belief as a result of this pivotal incident in his childhood.

This is exactly the sort of thing that we should be alert to in our own lives. In many ways, our past traumas and hurts are valuable portals for us now. Many people don't like to revisit negative events in their lives, but there can be a positive purpose in doing so, as long as it's not overly re-traumatizing. If we can go back mainly for the purpose of identifying limiting beliefs that we may have taken on at the time, then we can choose to overwrite those beliefs and thus transform our present and future reality for the better.

Digging Deep

1. Do you regularly watch the news or read the newspapers? If so, how do you think it affects the way that you view the world?

2. How could you stay informed without playing into the negativity bias? What advice would you give to someone about that?

3. Where in your life do you feel that you have fears about scarcity? How has this affected some of the choices you have made or the way that you have lived your life?

4. How would it feel to live in a state of abundance? Is this something you have experienced?

5. Describe the times in your life when you have felt the most abundant.

Action Steps

1. Try disconnecting from all forms of TV, news, advertisements, newspapers, and online or other media for three days. Just try it. Unplug and see what

happens. Pay particular attention to your internal mind chatter. Try to notice if it changes or becomes a bit quieter over the course of those few days.

2. If you want to keep going for another three days, or even longer, start substituting your old choice of media consumption with viewing some of the inspiring talks on TED (www.ted.com) or from other reputable sources. Again, notice what, if anything, changes with respect to your internal mind chatter.

3. Introduce ten minutes of meditation into your daily routine. Try five minutes in the morning and five minutes in the evening of just being aware of your breath flowing into and out of your nostrils.[5] Let your thoughts pass across your mind like trains passing through a station. Simply notice them without participating in them—without hopping on the train, so to speak. If you notice that you have jumped onto a train of thought, just get off again, let it go, and return to focus on your breath. This can be a great way to become even more attuned to the nature of the internal chatter going on in your mind and to help quiet the mind to promote greater clarity of thought.

4. Visit www.theabundancecodebook.com to access some extra content about the 7 Money Myths that I have created for you.

CHAPTER FOUR

Money Myth #2: Time = Money

"Time Is Money"

The Scarcity Mind-Set is a way of thinking about things that is, by its very nature, limited. This second myth is an example of one of the beliefs that we use to impose limits on the amount of money we can make.

Many people believe that the ability to make money is linked in some inextricable way to the amount of time they put into it. They believe that if you want to get rich, you'll probably have to devote a lot of time to it.

If "time is money," then the ability to make money is inherently limited because there are only 24 hours in a day. And anyway, "Rome wasn't built in a day." Or so they say. Everything takes time, right?

Or does it?

Even though we have increasingly seen massive fortunes being built in relatively short time periods—like those of the founders of Facebook, Groupon, and Pinterest, for example—many people still believe that to become a millionaire requires long-term effort and intense dedication, a total devotion to the goal of becoming rich.

It's perhaps true enough that many self-made millionaires are workaholics. And it's also perhaps true that in their pursuit of wealth and status, many workaholics can end up compromising on the things that money can't buy—such as time to enjoy their life, contentment, a healthy work-life balance, strong family relationships, a fulfilling romantic partnership, and friendships with people who aren't interested in them just for their money.

But just because we can find examples of people who have made their money by devoting nearly all of their available time to the cause, that doesn't mean it has to go this way. There are plenty of other millionaires, and even billionaires, who have gotten rich by removing themselves from the *time* = *money* equation.

Take Donald Trump for example. He made his fortune by using his greatest assets: his twin skills of identifying property development opportunities and conducting deal negotiations. He was able to consistently use those skills to make massive amounts of money. It hasn't all been smooth sailing for him either. At one point, he was in debt to the tune of nearly a billion dollars! But he never lost faith in his skills and his moneymaking ability, and he was able to use those skills to get himself back on top.

For Trump, the real money is not in the time he puts in, although of course a lot of work goes into each deal. The real money is in finding the right deal and driving the right bargain.

Examine the Equation

Look at it this way: If all you ever do is exchange your time for money on an hourly basis, then the only way you'll be able to get wealthy is by charging a huge hourly fee. How realistic is that?

Hourly charging is certainly the business model of many professionals such as lawyers, doctors, and consultants. They give their time in exchange for money. In this model, it is usually their level of education that determines the hourly rate they can charge. The more education required in obtaining the skill they have (accountants, lawyers, surgeons, and the like), the higher the hourly rate.

But the long years of education have a cost that should also be factored in. Once you look at how much it costs in educational expenses to become a certified accountant, lawyer, or surgeon, plus how many hours have gone into the non-earning period while the person was acquiring the skill, the hourly rate doesn't look so fantastic anymore.

Economists call this the life-cycle model of income. It explains the seemingly huge incomes earned by highly skilled professionals later in life by showing the true cost of the foregone income they sacrificed and the expenses they incurred earlier in life in acquiring their skills.

The fact is that exchanging your time for money is always going to be a limited approach, no matter how smart or highly skilled you are. The restriction on the time-for-money approach is twofold:

1. There will probably be a limit on how much people are going to be willing to pay you for an hour of your time. This rate will largely be determined by the market demand for your services, as well as by the number of competing providers of a similar service to yours. So you won't be fully in control of what rate you can charge per hour.

2. There is a limit on how many hours you will be able to give. There are only 24 hours in a day, right? That's not a belief . . . that's a fact.

Why Might We Want to Believe "Time = Money"?

The belief about time being a crucial ingredient to wealth is important to many of us, because this is the belief that lets us off the hook if we are *not* wealthy. We can rationalize our mediocre asset base by saying we have prioritized other things in our lives above money—we have chosen to use our time in other ways.

This allows us to say that we don't have financial freedom because we have chosen instead to devote ourselves to our families and friends, for example, building good relationships. Maybe we have decided to spend time on relaxation or our own well-being, or possibly we have opted to pursue other interests outside the realm of paid work.

It is the belief in *time = money* that leads many of us to say, "I don't want to sacrifice my family or my lifestyle just to become rich. There's more to life than money."

Yes. There is more to life than money. Family, friends, and the pursuit of the things we feel passionate about are important ingredients for a happy life. But who says we have to sacrifice these things for financial freedom or money?

Usually, we are the ones who say that. Or at least, we are the ones who subconsciously believe it.

Working Smarter Not Harder

Prior to about the 1970s, single-income families were the norm, and one person's salary in the middle class was generally enough to provide a decent standard of living for the whole family. Over the last few decades, more and more families have discovered that a single income is no longer enough. Now, more than ever, we need to work smarter, not harder.

Global integration via the Internet, as well as cheaper and faster communications technology, is allowing all kinds of projects to be outsourced to suppliers in developing countries in a way we have never seen before. People in the industrialized world are now finding that they have to work harder and longer to maintain the same standard of living. And this shift is accelerating in pace.

In the corporate realm of multinational companies, labor's share of profits is purposefully bid down in order to bid up a company's share price. That is to say, the more profit that is retained by the company, and the less that's given to its workers, the higher the company's share price will tend to go. That's how senior executives command the big bucks: by delivering a rising share price. If they're not smart enough to do this by adding value, they'll do it by cutting costs. The really smart ones do both.

So we see an effort to keep labor costs down by downsizing, outsourcing projects, or moving entire operations to countries where labor is relatively cheap, and also by automating processes that were previously done manually, by people. These strategies benefit the senior executives through huge performance bonuses and the shareholders through a rising share price. But the average local worker is the one who often loses out in this equation.

If we interact with the world only as workers, we may soon realize that we face ever-increasing competition from a cheap workforce in developing countries—and not just in the area of unskilled labor, as some people assume. Even now in fields such as information technology, engineering, and chemistry, there is intense pressure to outsource work to other countries where these skills can be accessed inexpensively.

Won't Our Superior Skills Save Us?

Sometimes it's argued that workers in developed countries will retain an advantage over those in less-developed countries due to their superior skill levels. There is a commonly held notion that developing countries will take advantage of what they have in abundance—cheap but relatively unskilled labor—and that developed countries will remain dominant in what is called "value add" by using what they have in abundance: the skills and education of their workforce.

If we interact with the world only as workers, we may soon realize that we face ever-increasing competition from a cheap workforce in developing countries—and not just in the area of unskilled labor.

However, a look at some recent trends paints quite a different picture. First, the assumption that workers in developing countries have a lower level of education is just plain wrong. Take the examples of China and India (sometimes referred to as "Chindia" because they represent a powerful block of development that is driving huge amounts of change in the global marketplace). Together, these two developing countries have a larger population than all of the countries in the developed world *combined*. They both have plenty of cheap and competitive unskilled labor, but they also both boast reasonably high levels of education for a decent chunk of the population.

No one has been surprised that these countries are competitive in low-tech, labor-intensive industries such as textiles and manufacturing. However, what has surprised some people is their rise to prominence in high-tech domains that were previously dominated by countries of the developed world.

For example, in the last decade India has successfully become a serious rival to Silicon Valley in the realm of software development. Pretty much all of the major software firms now have operations in India, and in many cases India has become their main hub for software development. Due to a reasonably good education system that is highly accessible, even to the poor, Indian workers are in a position to excel in new fields of opportunity like computer programming.

China is also a leader in such high-tech domains as the semiconductor industry, biotechnology, engineering, industrial chemistry, and many other scientific disciplines. In China, there is an abundance of workers with a high standard of education and skills, especially in the areas of science and engineering, whose labor is much cheaper than that of workers in the developed world.

Workers in Western developed economies are finding that just having an undergraduate degree is no longer enough. Ground is rapidly being lost to developing nations and to the increasing use of automation in jobs that do not require an advanced degree.

In April 2012, a *New York Times* blogger quoted this report based on U.S. governmental data showing that in many cases, education was not helping college graduates to get better jobs:

> Broken down by occupation, young college graduates were heavily represented in jobs that require a high school diploma or less.
>
> In the last year, they were more likely to be employed as waiters, waitresses, bartenders and food-service helpers than as engineers, physicists, chemists and mathematicians combined (100,000 versus 90,000). There were more working in office-related jobs such as receptionist or payroll clerk than in all computer professional jobs (163,000 versus 100,000). More also were employed as cashiers, retail clerks and customer representatives than engineers (125,000 versus 80,000).
>
> According to government projections released last month, only three of the 30 occupations with the largest projected number of job openings by 2020 will require a bachelor's degree or higher to fill the position—teachers, college professors and accountants. Most job openings are in professions such as retail sales, fast food and truck driving, jobs which aren't easily replaced by computers.[1]

It's time to wake up and smell the coffee.

This is not the time to be arrogant and assume local jobs or even entire industries are safe from the pressures of the outside world. Make no mistake, the world is full of workers who are good at what they do, who are smart, and who are educated.

However, a lot of them have a distinct competitive advantage (if you can call it that): They are hungry for the kind of prosperity we take for granted in the developed world, so they are prepared to work harder and longer for less.

Continuing to believe *time = money* is the best way to get ahead is just a recipe for facing savage competition.

Now, I'm not trying to be negative. There's still a huge amount of opportunity in the world, and there are many ways to make money. But let's not be in denial about emerging trends. It's important to have a good look at the current reality, even if it's just so that you can reach a realistic assessment about where future possibilities might lie.

What I'm arguing here is that interacting with the world only as a worker is *not* a good strategy. Blindly assuming that the *time = money* model will stand you in good stead probably isn't smart. Look at the way the world is now. Look at the way it is moving today and toward the future, instead of viewing it through an old-fashioned lens created to fit the world the way it was when your parents (or your parents' parents) grew up. They were probably taught that the *time = money* model works just fine. And maybe it still does, if you want to work hard, work long, and yet never have job security . . . as long as you don't really want true financial freedom.

Continuing to believe *time = money* is the best way to get ahead is just a recipe for facing savage competition, because it's a Scarcity Mind-Set. And that way of thinking is all about competition. If that's what you believe and that's the game you choose to play, then that's what tends to show up.

Here is my prediction: Increasingly, only those who take the road of leveraging their time and getting their money to work for them will see their standards of living rise.

Case Study: Barry

Barry's story illustrates how the shifting sands of global competition and technological change can impact directly on a person's livelihood.

Barry had a business based around repairing electronic equipment. The company had been in the family for a long time—his father had started it. Barry began working there when he came of age. He learned the trade, and he eventually took over running it when his father retired.

He had a few overhead expenses: He employed a couple of technicians, he had some tools and technical equipment, he had a van for picking up and dropping off items for repair, and he rented the workshop space.

Once upon a time, it was a great little business. They repaired people's TVs, video players, stereos, and microwaves . . . basically any device that had an electrical fault. Some of it was warranty work; some of it was for items that were no longer under warranty, but it was still cheaper for people to get things fixed than it was to replace them. Most of the warranty work was also done because it was cheaper for the manufacturer to pay someone to repair the item than it was to replace it.

Barry did really good work, and he had a great reputation in the business. He worked long hours, and you could say that he was a really honest guy with a strong work ethic.

I think you probably know the end to this story. Most people know that these days, it's almost always cheaper to throw out the broken item and get a new one than it is to repair a TV, DVD player, or almost any other electronic device. The prices have plummeted, lowering the replacement costs, while at the same time the device complexity has increased, raising the repair costs.

Eventually, Barry saw the writing on the wall and decided to sell his business while he could still find a buyer and before the business went into debt. He didn't get much for it, but he was able to offload the overheads and the responsibility for all of the company's expenses, and he was hired back by the new owner to continue to work there for a wage.

Ordinarily, this would not be a particularly good outcome in return for a solid couple of decades of hard work. Over the years, running the business had meant very little holiday time for Barry and plenty of stress. So he might have felt pretty crushed to get so little for an enterprise he had dedicated so much time to.

Luckily, though, he had already started the process of freeing himself from the *time* = *money* equation. Both Barry and his wife had wisely set aside a portion of their incomes, and they had used that money to buy an investment property in addition to their family home. Later, they also bought the commercial premises that the workshop was running out of.

Because of this, Barry is content knowing that for now he has both a job (an income stream) and a cushion of assets from his investments, and he no longer has to be responsible for running a business that has little future. Having that investment cushion made the decision to get out of the business a lot easier for him and his wife.

Barry still likes the work, and he really likes having offloaded the stress of managing the business and its employees. He's started whistling, smiling, and cracking jokes again, instead of looking pale and gray all the time from stress.

If the business does go bust under the new management, Barry will be out of a job. But he probably won't go bankrupt, because he'll still have the cushion of the value of his investments. The main thing he has to keep an eye on is that the new owners make their rent on the workshop space, because he is the landlord of that property.

Barry has more time now because he doesn't always have to pick up the slack when one of the other technicians is sick or on holiday, so he can use that time to retrain in another field. And thanks to the fact that Barry and his wife had invested in property, they were not so devastated when the electronics-repair business first went into decline. They feel that they were probably more clearheaded about knowing when to get out because they weren't desperate.

Free Yourself from "Time = Money"

The key to freeing yourself from the *time = money* constraint is to open your mind to another way. The goal is to eventually get yourself to the point where you will no longer need to exchange your time for money in order to live comfortably.

Start thinking about how you can get your cash working for you. Set aside some of your income and invest it in a way that it will work for you and give you more time in the future.

Develop Passive and Scalable Income

If you want to eventually free yourself from the need to exchange your time for money, then one of the best ways to achieve this is to invest your money so that it delivers relatively passive or scalable income streams. What do I mean by this? Passive income streams only require a very small, hopefully fixed, time commitment on your part to be set in motion. And scalability means it shouldn't necessarily require any more effort if you decide to engage more capital. Here are some examples of passive income investments:

- **Term deposits:** You invest some cash, usually with a bank, for a fixed time period (usually between 3 and 12 months) with a pre-agreed and fixed rate of interest. Once you set up a term deposit, it will deliver a predetermined rate of return on your money. And setting up a term deposit for a large amount of money is no more work than it is for a small amount.

- **Bonds:** These are similar to term deposits in that you invest cash for a fixed time period with a pre-agreed and fixed rate of return. The main difference is that the term of the investment is usually longer—from 12 months up to 10, 20, or even 30 years in some cases. Also, most bonds tend to be issued by governments instead of banks.

- **Rental income:** Money earned by renting out a property that you own. Once you have purchased the property, rented it out, and installed a rental-property manager, the property should produce a regular income with very little time investment required on your part.

I've found that well-selected residential property in an emerging or gentrifying neighborhood with a good rental return and solid tenancy rates is an excellent addition to any investment portfolio. Commercial property can also be great because its rental returns are often higher than for residential property, and the lease terms are often longer as well (three to five years in many cases).

The main difficulty with investment property is the need to have a big enough deposit to start with, in order to ensure that the rent covers the mortgage. You also should have some contingency planning in place in case mortgage interest rates rise or the tenants default on their rent. Mortgage and landlord insurance are available to help cover these risks.

Another advantage of investment property is that it can allow you to access both income and potential capital gains.

Aim for Income and Capital Gain

If you wish to free yourself from the *time = money* constraint and grow your wealth overall, it's good to focus on both income and capital gain.

A focus only on capital gain could find you in a position of being asset rich but cash poor. This often happens when people overinvest in their own homes, for which they receive no rental income stream. They may have a valuable asset in their home, but they still find that they have to exchange their time for money because that asset doesn't provide them with any income. They can only access the value tied up in that asset—and access greater freedom for themselves—if they sell the asset or increase the mortgage on it. And that can lead to *less* freedom, not *more*.

A focus purely on income, however, can also be less than optimal when it comes to investing. A term deposit, for example, will only provide interest income, not capital gains. The "capital" is the amount of cash you have invested in the term deposit. With a term deposit there is no change in the total cash invested, unless you reinvest the interest earnings when the term deposit matures—that is, if you roll the original investment plus the interest earnings over into another term deposit.

If you wish to free yourself from the *time = money* constraint and grow your wealth overall, it's good to focus on both income and capital gain.

There is no capital-gain component to a cash term-deposit investment. In fact, the real value of the term-deposit investment capital will tend to erode over time due to inflation.

We measure the value of our cash by how much it can buy. Economists call this "purchasing power." Inflation means that over time your cash will buy less and less. That means inflation actually erodes the real value of your cash when measured in terms of your purchasing power.

The best you can do with a term deposit is to make sure the interest rate you're receiving is higher than the inflation rate, and possibly reinvest some of the interest income in order to access compounding returns over time (I'll talk more about compounding returns in Chapter 6).

An investment property, on the other hand, could provide both income and capital gains. If the rent on the property more than covers the mortgage payments, this is a regular income stream. And if the property value rises over time, it provides a capital gain on the investment.

Hopefully your investment strategy will allow for a gain in the overall asset value of the investment, as well as providing a regular income stream.

Become a Business Owner

Another way to detach from the *time = money* constraint is to run your own business and leverage your time by having employees who work for you.

This can be great if you choose a business in one of your areas of expertise, where you understand both the opportunities and the risks. It can also be easier said than done, though, because running a business can sometimes end up giving you the *opposite* of the freedom you desire.

It's something to be careful about. I've certainly had mixed experiences when it comes to running businesses, and I've learned some harsh lessons. However, mostly I've found that business can be a great way to leverage yourself and detach from the *time = money* constraint.

Case Study: Soap Opera School

While I lived in Japan, I ran my first business, which was a small school teaching English as a second language (ESL). I bought the enterprise, which was already a going concern, together with a business partner. We had a couple of employees, and most of our English students were young undergraduates who were studying at the university campus situated near our school.

After taking over and running the English school for a few months, my partner and I realized that the number one revenue-leverage area in the business was student retention. It took a lot of promotional effort, time, and money to get a new student in the door. So anything we could do to keep that student coming back was going to have a big dividend for the business in the long run.

I'd already learned Japanese as my second language, and I felt that I understood what it was like to be a young language student. I'd really hated the boring textbooks that we'd been forced to study. They'd taught me the basics of vocabulary and grammar, but very little about the kind of Japanese that young people actually spoke.

My progress in conversational Japanese was very slow by that method, even though I was living in Japan and immersed in the culture. I ended up learning most of my spoken Japanese by taking a job at night working in a bar.

By university age, most Japanese students have been studying English for several years. They can actually read it quite well at that point, their vocabulary is pretty good, and they have a decent grasp of English grammar. What they can't do, generally, is have a conversation. That's where our students needed help: in understanding spoken English and knowing how to join conversations.

We decided to throw out the boring old textbooks and develop an entirely new multimedia curriculum focused around the kind of English that is actually spoken by young people. We wanted to show our students not only how the language works when written down, but also how it sounds when spoken, and to show videos of how it's used in context. And we wanted it to be contemporary—English actually in use by young people, including slang. So we decided to base the curriculum around a TV show.

Japanese generally want to learn English with an American accent, so we selected a popular American TV show at the time (in the '90s): *Melrose Place*. We got recordings of the show that were in English, but also had English subtitles. Then we created a transcript of each episode and built lesson plans around that to explain the phrases used and to give examples of other contexts where similar expressions might be used in spoken English.

Each hour-long episode (45 minutes without the ads) ended up breaking down into three one-hour English lessons. We would go over a section of the transcript that covered about 15 minutes of the episode. Next, the class would watch it on video. Then we would discuss it and do some situational role-plays. Finally, we would watch the segment again.

This is when I stumbled upon one of the key principles of the Abundance Mind-Set: *Have fun!* I've noticed that when I'm having fun and focusing on being of service to others—both of which were key motivations in this case—that's when abundance flows into my life a lot more easily.

The *Melrose Place* method, as I like to call it, turned out to be a much more fun way to teach English than using the boring textbooks we had inherited with the business. Our students loved it because they were having fun, too! And they learned how to converse in English a lot more easily. Their progress by this method was much faster.

As a bonus, we no longer had a retention problem. Our students became so addicted to the show that they would never miss a class—because they couldn't wait to find out what happened next!

Soon the business was doing really well, and word of mouth was spreading, thereby cutting our promotional costs way down. Our school was popular, and we all loved teaching the curriculum. Since *Melrose Place* ran for seven seasons and each episode took us three lessons to cover, we weren't going to run out of material for years!

The *Melrose Place* method ticked all the boxes: It was fun, it was effective, and it improved student retention. And we were prosperous as a result.

When I finished my studies in Japan and was ready to come back to Australia, I sold my half of the business to my partner. He continued to run the school and prosper from it for many years after. And I ended up with a sizable deposit for my first investment property.

If I Detach from "Time = Money" . . . Then What?

What happens after you no longer need to exchange your time for money in order to get by? Once your money is working for you and providing you with a passive income stream that meets your needs and provides you with the kind of lifestyle you want . . . what will you do with all the time you suddenly have on your hands?

Well, whatever you want. And if you still want to do some time-for-money exchange just because you enjoy what you do, then that's fine. You still can. You can do whatever you want. You're free.

So are you done, then?

Well, as it turns out, freeing yourself from the *time = money* constraint can kick up a whole new layer of resistance: the belief that you have to work hard for your money in order to deserve it. That's a myth I'll talk about in detail in the next chapter.

Digging Deep

1. Have you ever felt limited by the *time = money* approach to wealth creation? If so, how?

2. What percentage of your current income comes from exchanging your time for money? By this I mean an hourly rate payment or salary.

3. What percentage of your income comes from revenue streams where your money works for you and makes you more money (with relatively little time investment required from you)?

4. What percentage of your total wealth is invested in assets that are likely to increase in value over time (in other words, experience capital gains)? How sure are you that these assets are going to rise in value? What mechanisms do you have in place to protect your investment capital against downside risks?

Action Steps

1. Write down your ideal lifestyle composition. What do you feel would be the ideal balance for you in terms of work that you enjoy, leisure, holidays, time with your family, personal development, and so on?

2. Make a list of ways you think that you could increase the proportion of passive income and capital gains from investments, and decrease the proportion of time-for-money exchange in your financial life. Even if you come up with some pretty wild and "out there" ways, don't edit yourself right now. Just brainstorm. You never know what brilliant ideas you might come up with!

3. Think for a moment about what kinds of things you really *love* doing. What kind of activity do you find so absorbing that it makes you lose track of time? How can you incorporate more of that into your life?

4. Once you identify the thing (or things) that you *love* to do, ask yourself, *Could I make money doing this?* If not, it doesn't necessarily matter . . . that may not be the point. It's okay to do something just because you love it. But still, investigate the question.

5. Visit www.theabundancecodebook.com to access some extra content about the 7 Money Myths that I have created for you.

CHAPTER FIVE

Money Myth #3: Work = Worth
"You Have to Work Hard for Your Money"

Not only are we taught to believe that it takes hard work and long hours to make money, we are also taught to believe that hard work is the *only* legitimate way to build wealth. These ideas are the central tenets behind the so-called work ethic.

Because we're taught that it takes hard work to make money, we often find the prospect of losing or risking money really daunting. If we risk our "hard earned" cash on a venture, and we lose it . . . and if the only way we know how to get those funds back is by working hard . . . then the idea of risking money on anything becomes a prospect that can easily fill us with a sense of anxiety and fatigue.

Does Working Hard Make You a Good Person?

We are taught to respect those who have worked hard for what they have. A popular commendation of good character in Australia, for example, is "She's not afraid of hard work."

The work ethic invites us to believe that there is something noble in that which one has worked hard for. We are encouraged to do "an honest day's work for an honest day's pay." The implication is that good people work hard; honest people work hard.

So here we can see how working hard and having a good work ethic become subtly tied to our sense of being good, honest, or deserving. It also becomes a yardstick by which we measure and respect both others and ourselves.

On the flip side, we are suspicious of those who don't work hard. We suspect they are privileged, dishonest, or lazy.

The idea of doing an honest day's work is not a bad idea in itself. But just because we have been taught to believe in honesty, let's not fall into the trap of thinking that money that comes easily is somehow dishonest. We don't want to let the mind reject an easier path to wealth.

There is, I suspect, an underlying belief that we are not worthy of having money unless we've worked hard to get it. And there's a subtle companion to this as well: the belief that if we manage to come by wealth without working hard for it, this is somehow akin to cheating.

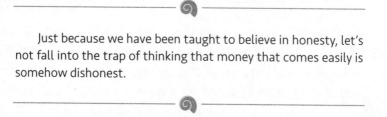

Just because we have been taught to believe in honesty, let's not fall into the trap of thinking that money that comes easily is somehow dishonest.

How Others Judge You

How often is it that when you meet someone new at a party or social gathering, the first thing they ask you is, "What do you do?" Is this just an accepted icebreaker that has little meaning, or does it tell us something important about the way we judge each other?

The first question you are asked at a party is not, "What do you do for fun?" or "What do you dream about?" or "What would you do in life if money was not a constraint?" No. People generally ask you for something that they can measure you by, and work is the first thing they often reach for as a standard.

On a deeper level, what they're probably asking is, "What are you worth to society?" or "What are you worth to our community?" or even "What might you be worth to *me?*" Sometimes it's also, "Where do you fit in society compared to me? Do I outrank you, or do you outrank me?"

We laugh about it now, but asking, "What's your star sign?"—popular in the '60s and '70s—was an attempt to move away from the "What are you worth?" type of question. The sexual and social revolution of those decades was about shedding the old societal norms and definitions of people, and allowing individuals to express themselves freely and openly. So it's not surprising that there was a move toward enquiring into the nature of the person as an individual rather than the nature of the person's position in a hierarchy or their contribution to society.

Now it seems that with the reemergence of a strong, career-oriented work ethic for both men and women, the focus is back on our position in society. It's back on "What do you do?"

These changes may seem subtle, but they say a lot about how we view ourselves, how we judge others, and what we believe. Do not underestimate how much you want to be seen as a worthwhile person. If having a good work ethic and working hard means being viewed as a good person, then can you understand how you could be very committed subconsciously to the idea of hard work?

If you want to be a good person, and you don't want to be seen by others as being lazy, then the simple answer is to work hard. But being this particular brand of "good" and being *happy* are not necessarily the same thing and may not even be compatible goals. If working hard were the simple answer to happiness, then we would see a world full of happy workers. And that is clearly not the case!

Do You Deserve Financial Freedom?

On a deep, subconscious level, the work ethic idea is tied up with working-class values about worthiness. It's about the connection we tend to make between our work and our worth.

As we are growing up, material gifts are often given according to a system of rewards and taken away in punishment. If we are good, we get to eat cake, go to the movies, and receive the things on our Christmas list. If we aren't so good, we might not get those things. And if we are really naughty, we might have some things taken away from us! In this way, material prosperity is tied to our sense of being good enough. And as we get older, society continues to subtly ask us to prove ourselves worthy of what we receive in life.

This myth is not just a belief about the way things work, but also a belief about how they *should* work—it's about what we think is right. There is a layer of judgment concealed in this myth. The judgment about being worthy of wealth and financial freedom can go a bit like this:

- Maybe you deserve it because you worked hard for it . . .

- Maybe you deserve it because you suffered and sacrificed . . .

- Maybe you deserve it because you are a good Christian, Jew, Muslim, or Hindu (or whatever your belief system may be), and God knows you deserve it so he or she has blessed you with it . . .

- *But* if you got it any other way—especially if that way was really easy—then you probably *don't* deserve it . . .

- And if you don't deserve it, you shouldn't have it!

On the other hand, if we manage to get ahead in life by following the work ethic, then we get to wear it like a badge of honor. The work ethic becomes our rite of passage. We can feel that we have the right to be prosperous because we worked hard. We played the game by the rules and won. Fair enough.

I worked hard to get where I am in life, so I deserve it. This is what our society teaches; what the majority of people in our parents' generation believed, and their parents' generation; and what many of us have subconsciously accepted. It's quite possible that we are unconsciously teaching our children to believe it as well.

We really have to look at this idea of being *deserving*. It runs deep in our society and throughout our religious traditions. It is the belief that in order to deserve what you have, then you must have done something "worthy."

Significance and Contribution

Significance and contribution are important things to human beings. According to self-help guru Anthony Robbins, people have six fundamental emotional needs:

1. Certainty
2. Variety
3. Significance
4. Love (Connection)
5. Growth
6. Contribution

These things are very important to us; and given that, I would argue that they affect how we judge ourselves and others.

It's hard to come to a judgment about the level of certainty, variety, love, connection, or growth in another person's life; and we tend to view these things as more private matters. So I believe that when we are trying to assess others, we most often reach for yardsticks that represent significance and contribution. Others tend to judge us in this manner also.

Therefore it's not surprising that people take a lot of pride in what they do. Many even attach a large part of their personal sense of worth to what they do and how well they do it. Their professional life is where they gain most of their sense of significance and contribution. With a good level of professional success, they feel more confident that they will be judged well by those around them, and they are more likely to judge themselves well.

Case Study: David

David was a highly respected surgeon for his entire working life. His job was, of course, very stressful because he was taking people's lives in his hands every day.

When David retired from his high-stakes work, he expected to feel less pressure. To his surprise, however, he found that after he retired his level of stress went *up* not down. He was stressed about different things, of course, but he was certainly not having the relaxed retirement he'd expected. David actually suffered a stress-related illness because of this. Why was this happening?

David had lost his sense of significance and contribution, and because of that he felt completely at sea. It was not until he found a way to replace that sense of significance and contribution that his stress levels dropped. He did so by learning how to invest in the stock market and by taking over the investment of his retirement funds.

He then felt that he could continue providing well for himself and his wife, and he even started helping his children invest for their financial futures. His sense of contribution and significance returned. David once again saw himself as a productive and contributing member of his family.

Significance Is . . . Wherever You Find It

True financial freedom will mean that you no longer have to work for money. That may seem like the Holy Grail to you right now. But will this lack of work deprive you of your sense of significance and contribution?

It may give you the freedom to ask yourself, *What do I want to do for fun? What do I dream about?* and *Where do I want to go today?* But it is not going to stop others from asking, "So, what do you do?" and subtly judging you by the answer. And it might not stop you from judging yourself.

I'm not here to sit in judgment about who deserves money and who doesn't. In fact, in my opinion, everyone deserves financial freedom just as everyone deserves to be loved. In an ideal world, the question of deservedness would not even be raised. But in our world, it often is.

If you make a lot of money relatively easily, without working hard for it, then the question of whether or not you deserve it will probably be raised.

Most people still view wealth within the paradigm of scarcity and the work ethic, and most people believe that you have to do something to deserve what you've got. So you may have to face the judgment of your family members or friends if you suddenly try to break out of that mold.

If you make a lot of money relatively easily, without working hard for it, then the question of whether or not you deserve it will probably be raised. Others may be critical of you, and they may feel that you don't deserve financial freedom without working hard for it. *You* may even feel that you don't deserve it. And if you believe that, then you can rest assured that soon enough you won't have it anymore.

It can be quite tempting to stay where you are and not upset the applecart of beliefs. And it's not just what *you* believe, but also the beliefs and judgments of others—the people you associate with—that can have a powerful effect on you. If you want to be different from the pack, you will need the courage to be different. You will need to get to a place psychologically where you can handle being different.

The thing we need to be aware of is that many of us hold ourselves back from moving away from the work-ethic framework because subconsciously, we're afraid that we might not know how to find a sense of significance and contribution outside of that paradigm. These basic human psychological needs are not going away, no matter what your financial circumstances are. So in order to move away from the work-ethic paradigm, it's a good idea to establish an alternative sense of significance and contribution. Find other ways to satisfy the need.

Robert Kiyosaki, the author of *Rich Dad Poor Dad* and numerous other financial-advice books, talks a lot about the importance of achieving financial freedom through what he calls "building a financial ark." In one of his books, Kiyosaki comments:

> One of the biggest surprises in my life was to finally become financially free. I had always thought that once I had enough money I could retire, sit on my ark, and take life easy. In 1994 at the age of forty-seven I finally completed the ark. Then I found out how boring life was just sitting on my ark . . .[1]

He goes on to touch on his own need for significance and contribution:

> In 1997 *Rich Dad Poor Dad,* the first in the Rich Dad series, was published with the assistance of my business partner, Sharon Lechter, who took my notes and transformed them into a book. Today we are busier than ever, sometimes longing for those days of boredom sitting on the ark, but nonetheless, I am grateful for the opportunity to be productive and contributing to society again.[2]

Kiyosaki experienced firsthand exactly what we are talking about. He discovered the fact that even after you gain financial freedom, the human need to feel a sense of significance and contribution does not suddenly disappear.

But you *can* transfer your source of significance and contribution from the work you do for money to the work you do for love. That "work" could be spending more time with your family, raising your children. Or maybe it could be exploring your creative side, doing volunteer work, or helping others. Sharing your inner gifts with others is one of the best ways to feel a sense of significance and contribution.

These are not trivial concerns. To feel that we deserve what we have, to feel a sense of significance and contribution—these things are very important to us as human beings.

Case Study: At Sea Without a Compass

In 1997, I quit my job. It was a good job as an economist and currency-markets researcher at the Reserve Bank of Australia. This was seen as the premier training ground for professional economists in the country. If you wanted a career as an economist, even if you planned to make your way eventually into the more highly paid sphere of investment banking, the Reserve Bank was where you needed to cut your teeth.

They'd recruited me from university in 1988. And they'd already taken me back once, after I'd gotten a scholarship and taken time out to complete my master's in finance and business administration in Japan. They weren't going to take me back again—I knew that. And at the time I didn't have another job that I was going to. I didn't even really have a clear plan. I just felt like I wasn't heading in the right direction in my life. I felt I was stuck in the rat race.

I'd had a taste of what it was like to run my own business and to disconnect from the *time = money* equation while I'd lived in Japan. I felt there had to be a better and less limited way forward for me than committing myself to a life on the hamster wheel. I'm sorry for mixing rodent metaphors, but you get the idea!

Many of my friends and family members thought I was making a supremely stupid decision in quitting that job, especially without having the next position lined up. They asked, Couldn't I just figure out a better direction *and* keep my job at the same time?

I didn't feel as though I could.

I'm sure you know what it's like: Even if a job doesn't feel like quite the right thing for you, time can just get chewed up in the daily grind. You get up, go to work, come home, fix dinner, put in a load of washing, hop online for a while or maybe watch some TV, and then it's time to go to bed. You try to fit in some exercise during the week and catch up with friends on the weekend . . . go on holidays occasionally . . . and before you know it, a year or two or three have passed, and nothing much has changed in your life.

I didn't want to just get stuck in that pattern. I knew I had to shake things up to break myself out of it. So I quit. I decided to live off my savings for a while and try to get my head clear about the next step.

To fill my days, I did some volunteer work. I went to the beach. I went to India for an extended holiday. Overall, I just did very little in the way of work-ethic type activity. I stayed out of work (and not even seeking work) for more than a year.

You might think, *Great! A long holiday! I would love that!*

Well, you probably would love it for a while. But you might also be surprised by what comes up emotionally as the weeks turn into months . . . and months. Giving up my sense of significance and contribution for such an extended period of time, with nothing really concrete on the horizon, was actually very challenging for me.

Without a strong sense of significance and contribution to society, it can be difficult to maintain self-esteem. This loss of self-esteem often happens to those who suddenly find themselves unemployed. Some people find it surprising that it also often happens to many individuals when they retire, as was the case for David, whose story you just read.

The movie *About Schmidt* also explored this issue. Jack Nicholson's character retires, loses his wife, and thereby loses all of his sources of significance and contribution. His kids are grown. He no longer has anyone depending on him or needing him. So what is he worth? Where is his value? His ensuing search for a sense of significance and contribution is a key theme of the film.

I quit my job at the Reserve Bank when I was 30 years old. Maybe I was having an early midlife crisis of sorts. I was at an age when I should have been gaining momentum in my career, not losing steam! And I experienced a strange sense of guilt about taking so much time off, when all I seemed to have to justify it was a vague sense of discontent.

Looking back, I'm glad I did it. It was an important period of reflection. I realized that even though I'd had a great job, I was never really going to get ahead as much or as quickly as I wanted by just exchanging my time for money. That was one of two major realizations I had during that period, and it got me thinking about how I could do things differently moving forward, which was the first step in making a change.

But at the time, I found it difficult to stay with the conviction that I was doing the right thing. Although it was nice to be free from having to go to work five days a week, I felt a lot like a ship at sea without a compass. What should I do to feel worthwhile? How could I feel significant? And how would I answer the dreaded party question, "So, what do you do?"

The question did indeed become a dreaded one, because how could I explain myself? I probably worried about other people's opinions a lot more back then than I do now. But I think most of us, when we really dig down, care what other people think. I worried about how people would judge me by my answer. At first, I answered by saying what I formerly did: "I was an economist, but now I'm taking some time off." Then I realized that this opened a whole new can of worms in the form of the next question: "Oh really? Why?"

I found that people seemed to react curiously to my answer, "I'm just taking some time off to try to figure out what I want to do with my life." Somehow that didn't seem, to many people, to be a *worthwhile* pursuit. Not at my age, anyway. I saw the quick judgment in the eyes of strangers: *lazy, self-involved, selfish.* At least, that's what I believed I saw.

Soon, I began to answer the "What do you do?" question by talking about my volunteer work. Well, that went down better. It was worthwhile in the eyes of others, and maybe even commendable. Much better to focus on that because it made it seem as if I were following some sort of altruistic higher calling. But the truth was that my volunteering was only part-time, and I really was just taking some time to figure out what I wanted to do with my life. The volunteer-work answer may have gone down better, but it felt a bit dishonest.

Eventually, I realized what I was doing. I was connecting my sense of self-worth to *what I did,* not *who I was.* That was my second major realization.

I had done it somewhat automatically when I'd been working. I'd had a highly respectable job, so it was easy to derive a sense of significance from that. But without that position, my need to attach my worth to what I was doing suddenly became more obvious to me.

Eventually, I realized what I was doing. I was connecting my sense of self-worth to *what I did,* not *who I was.*

As a means of weaning myself off the idea that my work equaled my worth, I challenged myself to become comfortable with answering the question "What do you do?" with a simple statement: "Nothing. I'm not really doing anything at the moment."

This did seem to make some people uncomfortable. But eventually I came to feel okay with it. That was just their reaction, I decided. The reactions of other people were simply indicative of their own beliefs, and I realized their discomfort at not having a yardstick to measure me by didn't really say anything about me as a person, nor did it say anything about my inherent worthiness.

As a bonus, once we got past the fixation of talking about "what we do," the conversations I ended up having were much more meaningful and interesting.

Are You Worth It?

If you really want to have financial freedom, then first you have to be able to answer this question: Do you believe you deserve it? Do you feel worthy of it? Do you feel it in the core of your being? Because if you don't, then you most likely won't let yourself have it.

So if you are planning on parashifting, and you do want to escape the rat race and attain financial freedom, then pay some attention to the way in which you derive your sense of significance and contribution, because that will need to shift as well. The trick is to derive a strong enough alternative sense of significance and contribution, and to get comfortable enough with your own sense of self-worth, that you can transition easily from the path society has conditioned you for onto your own path—one that you find freer and more fulfilling.

The great news is that financial freedom means that we can get our personal sense of significance and contribution from wherever we want. Freeing ourselves from what we *have to do* is what gives us both the opportunity (and the need) to find out what we *want to do.* By freeing ourselves from the game that everyone else is playing, we can discover a new and even more fulfilling way to play.

Digging Deep

1. Do you think you feel more satisfied about what you have earned or what you have achieved when you've had to work hard for it?

2. Does this sense of satisfaction apply only to things you do for money or also to things you might put effort toward, but you're not necessarily paid for?

3. Have you ever felt that you've attached your personal sense of significance, worth, or contribution to what you do for work or how hard you have worked?

4. Have you ever had an extended period off work,
    by your own choice or otherwise? If so, how did
    that affect your own sense of significance and
    contribution? Was there any impact on your self-
    esteem as result?

Action Steps

1. List some of your achievements or contributions in
    life that have made you feel good about yourself. Is
    there a common theme? If you can find a common
    theme, it may point to one of the driving forces in
    your life: your inner "why." This is kind of like your
    mission or inner purpose. The things you achieve
    when you are following your inner why bring with
    them a deep, almost spiritual, sense of satisfaction.

2. List some things that you would like to spend
    more time doing, if you could, that you think you
    would gain a sense of satisfaction, significance, or
    contribution from.

3. The next time you go to a party, try asking your
    conversation partners more questions about what
    makes them tick, what their passions are, what makes
    them want to jump out of bed in the morning, and
    what makes their hearts sing . . . and fewer questions
    about what they do. Also be aware of the tendency
    to talk about the weather or the news—not that you
    have to avoid these topics, but be aware that they're
    often not the best means of connecting with other
    people.

4. When someone at a party or any social occasion
    asks you, "What do you do?" try to answer simply
    and quickly. Then steer the conversation on to

interests, passions, and more fascinating topics that you can both connect around (unless you happen to be passionate about what you do, in which case, go ahead and talk about it to your heart's content!).

5. Visit www.theabundancecodebook.com to access some extra content about the 7 Money Myths that I have created for you.

CHAPTER SIX

Money Myth #4: It Takes Money to Make Money

"The Rich Get Richer, While the Poor Get Poorer"

Not everyone is born to privilege, and those of us who are not "to the manor born" may have been subtly programmed to believe that true wealth and financial independence are somehow out of reach—that is, unless you work very hard for a very long time. "The rich get richer, while the poor get poorer," we are told, as if abundant wealth is some kind of closed-door club to which people can only be granted access by virtue of birth or luck.

The first three myths that we've looked at pave the way, psychologically, for this fourth belief. The *scarcity* belief conditions us to settle for less and to be fearful of losing what little we've got because "money doesn't grow on trees." The *time = money* and *work = worth* beliefs condition us to accept that we will have to work very hard for a very long time if we want to get ahead.

The implication is this: Exchange your limited hours each day for a limited amount of money, stick to it all your life, watch your pennies, live frugally, and one day you might reach a modest level of comfort . . . but you probably won't achieve great wealth or financial freedom. Subconsciously, this kind of programming tells you that it is useless to try to change your lot in life.

But why must that be so? Well, just in case you do start to question that, this fourth myth steps in with a ready answer: "It takes money to make money."

This myth tells us why we should forget about trying to attain financial freedom quickly and easily, and why we should probably even stop wanting it. It says that abundant wealth is the exclusive domain of those who already have it and is out of reach for anyone who is not either extremely lucky or born into it.

I know, it sounds silly—at least it sounds silly to me. But maybe that's because I no longer believe it. Yet many people do believe that "the rich get richer, and the poor get poorer" . . . at least subconsciously. A symptom that you might be carrying this kind of programming is if you are not allowing yourself to dream big or to want things that you think you can't have.

Out of Mind . . . Out of Reach?

I recently had a conversation with a friend who is going for a big promotion at work. He is incredibly talented and competent at his job, and he has recently been on a roll, kicking some major goals. As a result, he's been getting a lot of well-earned praise and recognition from his superiors.

I asked him what he thought his chances were of getting the promotion he wants.

"Oh, probably 50-50," he said.

To which I replied, "Come on! You've been rocking it lately. Surely your chances are better than that!"

"Okay," he said. "My chances probably are better than that . . . but I don't want to get my hopes up too much in case I don't get it."

Have you ever done something like that? Studies have shown that people do indeed suppress their desire for things that they fear might be out of reach.

If we can't see ourselves having success, money, financial freedom, or anything else we want . . . then we probably won't have them.

An August 2012 study by the University of New South Wales that surveyed children from poor and disadvantaged backgrounds in Australia showed that these children exhibit a phenomenon known as *adapted preferences:*

> Many participants who had experienced ongoing economic disadvantage expressed a narrow range of desires and interests. Adapted preferences is a phrase used to refer to the tendency to deny that one wants things that one cannot have, and that others consider customary. The evidence suggests that where young people regularly experienced the pain of missing out on experiences and activities accessible to their peers, they narrowed their interests and desires as a mechanism of self-protection or to protect their parents from the anguish of having to say "no."[1]

Our socioeconomic background can have a powerful effect on what we allow ourselves to want. This can mean that if we do not happen to come from a background of abundant wealth or financial freedom, we may have conditioned ourselves *to not even want it!*

Narrowing our desires may help us not to feel so dissatisfied with our lot in life, but it also prevents us from accessing and enjoying the boundless opportunities available. Not allowing ourselves to dream or to want big things can become a powerful habit that exerts an influence on the way we think, even when opportunities for success are available. Because if we don't actively want something, chances are we may not be actively seeking it. And if we're not actively seeking it . . . well, we have a lot less chance of getting it.

Take the case of my friend. There is absolutely no reason why he should not get that promotion. But how many little choices or opportunities to cement his chances of success might he miss seeing just because he doesn't want to focus on it too much for fear of getting his hopes up?

Remember the influence of the reticular activating system? If my friend does not tell his brain to sort the information it's receiving for extra opportunities where he could say or do things to increase his chances of getting the promotion, then his brain simply will not see those opportunities—even if they are right in front of him.

Sure, he might get the promotion anyway. I hope he does. And I certainly counseled him on the importance of believing that he will. But I hope you see my point: If we are not in the habit of being awake to (and actively seeking) greater possibilities in our lives, many opportunities will pass us by without our even noticing them.

There are a lot of little choices we make along the way that can heavily influence the outcomes we see in our lives. At the risk of oversimplification, it pretty much comes down to this: If we can't see ourselves having success, money, financial freedom, or anything else we want . . . then we probably won't have them.

The True Advantage of the Rich

Is it really the case that the rich get richer? Often, yes it is. The rich are generally investors, and they have often built up multiple passive streams of income. Generating relatively passive income, investing for a positive return, and compounding those returns are what the rich tend to understand quite well.

I'll talk more about the importance of compounding returns a little later on. But basically as time passes, income just keeps on rolling in and adding up, compounding and growing. Even after the rich die, their investment portfolios can keep on making money. For example, the estate of Elvis Presley has made 100 times more money than Elvis ever did when he was alive, largely because of passive income streams from royalties. Michael Jackson's estate will probably do the same.

There are many massive "old money" fortunes of families in the U.K., Europe, and the U.S., who have large holdings of real estate; portfolios of resources like gold, oil, or coal; shipping and other transportation assets; and telecommunications and media empires, to mention just a few sources of income and capital gain.

However, beyond just having an understanding of how to get their money working for them, those who are accustomed to having wealth also possess two distinct psychological advantages when it comes to creating more wealth:

1. They are not hobbled by belief in the work ethic (the twin myths of *time = money* and *work = worth*). The wealthy know that hard work is not the *only* way to generate wealth. In fact, they know that it is actually a very *limited* way to generate wealth. There are only 24 hours in a day, and one person can only do so much. The truly wealthy understand that the key to making a lot of money is to turn the work ethic on its head: Stop simply working hard for your money and instead make sure that your *money* is working hard for *you!*

2. The wealthy often have an innate sense of "deserving." In this instance I'm talking about people with generations of wealth in their family, not self-made millionaires. Very few old-money people are troubled by the idea that they might not *deserve* what they've got. They were born wealthy, their parents were wealthy, and often their parents' parents were wealthy. Wealth is a given for them—it's just a part of the way things are. It's not tied to any notion of having to be good or having to do something to deserve it. Nor do they feel the need, generally, to justify their wealth through hard work. They feel free to turn their attention and energy toward activities that they find rewarding and fulfilling.

The work ethic is a particularly working-class and middle-class way of thinking. Amongst the old-money wealthy, there can even be a certain disdain for those who have had to work for their money rather than having been born into it. As Robert Kiyosaki famously pointed out in his book *Rich Dad Poor Dad*, the rich have more than just material wealth. They tend to also have the advantage of an inherently wealthy mind-set. This can make all the difference.

So what if you do want to change your financial lot in life? Obviously, overwriting the scarcity belief and the work-ethic beliefs is going to be important. But these are not the only psychological barriers you might face.

Who Wants to Be a Fish Out of Water?

Most of us tend to view ourselves, either consciously or unconsciously, as belonging to a particular socioeconomic class or group of people: our "tribe."

There is a culture that we have been raised in, and usually a large part of that culture is organized around socioeconomic boundaries. Within these boundaries we find a sense of cultural belonging, and this sense of belonging is extremely important to us.

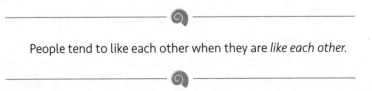

People tend to like each other when they are *like each other.*

Even if we think we are individuals and that it's not that important to belong to a tribe—it is. Having a sense of belonging with a group helps us define who we are and how to be in the world. It becomes part of our identity. We understand within this cultural frame of reference what is acceptable and what is not. And this understanding makes us feel comfortable.

As human beings, the need to belong to a "tribe" is fundamental to our sense of well-being. People tend to like each other when they are *like each other.* Consequently, the people around you can become uncomfortable when you try to change because you are suddenly not so much like them anymore. This can cause unexpected reactions of hostility and even rejection.

So even though you may think that you want to attain financial freedom on a conscious level, if it means moving out of your comfort zone in terms of your sense of belonging to a tribe, then on a deeper level you may not really want to do that. You may have subconscious resistance to leaving your tribe. This conflict can cause subconscious sabotage with respect to your conscious goal of financial freedom. (You can review subconscious sabotage in detail in Chapter 2.)

It's hard to go out on a limb and step outside the group, and indeed not everyone in the group is going to applaud you for doing that. Some of the people around you could feel quite confronted, as most people like the status quo to be maintained. "Don't rock the boat" can be a surprisingly vehement sentiment, which you only find out when you do try to rock it.

Case Study: Marlene and Jane

Marlene and Jane were roommates years ago. They were similar ages and had similar incomes. They were both very intelligent, and they shared a lot of the same interests. Yet they fought constantly while they were living together. They had come from different socioeconomic backgrounds, and this caused a surprising amount of friction between them.

Marlene had grown up with money. Marlene's parents had grown up with money, and her parents' parents had grown up with money. Marlene was programmed as "wealthy."

Jane had grown up without much money. In fact, she had grown up in quite a disadvantaged family. Jane's parents had always worked hard but had only just managed to scrape by. There was never quite enough, even to cover her family's most basic needs. Jane's parents' parents had grown up in a similar state of poverty. Jane was programmed as "poor."

Even though Marlene was not being financially supported by her family at the time and didn't really have more income than Jane did, because of her background, her attitudes about money were very different to Jane's. Marlene always carried a lot of cash on her, for example, so that she didn't have to go to the bank very often. Carrying a lot of cash didn't seem strange to her. Jane, on the other hand, only ever carried a small amount of cash. Carrying a lot of cash around did seem strange—and somewhat risky—to Jane.

So when Jane and Marlene wanted to do something, Jane always needed to find a bank or ATM first because she never had enough money on her (this was in the days before point-of-sale electronic transactions were common). If they couldn't find a bank or ATM, or didn't have time to find one, Jane would need to borrow cash from Marlene to do whatever it was they wanted to do.

This drove Marlene a bit crazy. She couldn't understand why Jane didn't seem to recognize the pattern, and how inconvenient it was, and how it would make her life easier if she would simply adjust her behavior by carrying more cash. But Jane just wasn't programmed that way.

When Jane and Marlene would head off to do the shopping, they would inevitably end up at loggerheads as well. Marlene would want to stock up and buy lots of the imperishable things like toilet paper, tinned food, washing powder, and the like so that when they ran out of something, they wouldn't have to run to the shops. They'd already have that item in reserve at home.

Jane, on the other hand, only really liked to shop for that day's needs. Maybe that was because she felt that once the money was spent you couldn't get it back, and you never knew what else you might need the money for more urgently than 24 rolls of reserve toilet paper.

When Marlene used the washing machine, Jane used to get angry because she thought that Marlene should wipe the inside of the washing barrel dry with a rag after using the machine. Marlene had no idea why you would bother wiping out a washing machine—she'd never heard of such a thing in her life! But Jane explained that she'd been taught to wipe the inside of the machine dry so that it wouldn't rust. That way it would last a lifetime.

Marlene pointed out that the washing machine they had, a high-quality one that her parents had supplied, came with a stainless-steel barrel, and it was very unlikely that it would rust. Jane still thought it should be wiped. Marlene just couldn't see wiping out the washing machine as being important, and she didn't ever do it. So they fought about that.

When other people's beliefs don't match yours, it's like having people tell you that the sun revolves around the Earth, when you know it's actually the other way around.

Marlene noticed that Jane had a lot of judgments about people who had money. She felt Jane tended to assume that the only way people got a lot of money was by ripping other people off. Marlene suspected that Jane believed it was actually wrong to have more money than you needed. This came up fairly frequently, as Marlene had several wealthy acquaintances and family friends, many of whom she felt Jane treated with suspicion or even sometimes incivility.

To be fair, Jane wasn't the only one who saw things from a particular angle. Marlene had the attitude that some of Jane's friends and family members were a bit rough and narrow-minded, and consequently she avoided spending time with them. This hurt Jane's feelings, as she felt that Marlene was being a snob.

Eventually, Jane and Marlene stopped living together.

They stayed friends, but the friendship was always a tumultuous one. From the outside looking in, you might have wondered why they bothered since they so frequently had disagreements. Yet they shared a wicked sense of humor, and they'd had a lot of fun times together, so this was the glue that allowed them to struggle on with the tenuous balance in their friendship.

Many years later, Marlene inherited a substantial amount of money from her family. That event proved to be too much for the friendship. The balance was tipped, because not only did they come from widely different wealth backgrounds, the levels of income they had access to were suddenly also widely different.

Marlene said that after she came into her inheritance, Jane became more and more hostile toward her. The issues Jane and Marlene had were no different to the disagreements they'd always had—but suddenly they seemed intolerable to Jane.

Within 18 months of Marlene's inheritance, despite nearly 30 years of friendship, Jane and Marlene were no longer speaking.

Having the Courage of Your Convictions

Can you face the discomfort of embracing a new way of thinking about wealth when those around you haven't? Do you think your friends will be happy for you when you do well for yourself and start attracting financial success easily?

Don't count on it. They may decide you don't deserve it, and they may even resent you for it—all because it pushes their own buttons about money while triggering resistance within their own belief structures. You can try to share your new way of thinking with the people around you, but many of them will not want to hear. Their underlying beliefs may not allow them to hear. Not everyone is ready to let go of their inherited mind-set, such as the belief that you have to work hard for your money or that you have to have done something "worthy" to deserve what you've got. You might be ready, but your friends, family members, and peers may not be.

It can be frustrating when the people you care about aren't supportive of your new direction in life. It can be downright hurtful when they're critical or even hostile toward you because of it. Ask yourself, *How would I respond if I felt the judgment of others just because I wanted to take my life in a new direction and access abundant wealth? Could I handle it?*

If we want our lives to be different, then we have to start doing things differently. That seems obvious. However, what's not obvious, and what a lot of people aren't prepared for, is the fact that change can be met with resistance both from within and from without.

The internal resistance to change can be overcome by over-writing your inner beliefs to match your outer desires. But what can we do about the beliefs of others? Nothing, really . . . it's hard enough to alter your own beliefs, let alone those of others! You can't choose change on behalf of anyone else; they have to do that for themselves.

This is where you are going to need the courage of your con-victions. When other people's beliefs don't match yours, it's like having those individuals tell you that the sun revolves around the Earth, when you know that it's actually the other way around.

The Galileo Effect

Imagine what it was like for Galileo Galilei (1564–1642), the scientist who confirmed with observational data the hypothesis that the Earth revolves around the sun (a theory known as *helio-centricity*) and not vice versa, as everyone had previously believed. Instead of being applauded for his brilliance, Galileo was locked away for putting forward such a radical idea. Why? Because it challenged people's cherished worldview.

To the Catholic church at the time, the idea that the Earth was at the center of God's universe was a very important belief. They wanted to believe that God had arranged everything in the universe to revolve around us. The church didn't like this being challenged by Galileo's scientific findings. No matter how much scientific proof Galileo showed them, they continued to reject the idea because it was too frightening a concept for them to embrace. If the sun did *not* revolve around the Earth, then that meant the Earth was *not* the center of the universe, and that meant human beings were *not* placed at the center of God's creation.

Uh-oh! That idea was just too controversial for the church to accept. They didn't want to know about that. It challenged their core belief structure. It implied that their whole understanding of humanity's role in God's creation might be wrong. In 1633,

Catholic church leaders had Galileo interrogated and threatened with torture—he was taken to the dungeons and shown the instruments of torture that surely would be used on him if he did not recant, at which point he conceded—and thus the church forced him to retract his theories. He was then sentenced to house arrest for an indefinite term, which stayed in force until his death in 1641 or 1642. The work in which his heliocentric world view was put forward was not removed from the Vatican's list of banned books until 1835, and they didn't actually admit that Galileo had been right all along until 1992!

Being Comfortable with Being Awkward

It's natural for us to be afraid of being different, because instinctively we know that it's natural for others to be hostile to divergence from the norm—particularly if our differences threaten their core beliefs. In extreme cases, being different can lead to ostracism, exile, confinement, torture, and even death. We are not exactly programmed to want those things!

As you gain financial abundance, it may take a while until your new financial circumstances begin to feel normal.

Resistance to being different, to feeling awkward, can be an obstacle in the process of achieving financial freedom. This is because you know on some level that achieving financial freedom could mean losing your place in your existing social group or tribe, while not having yet found your footing in a new group.

When you attempt to change your position in the socioeconomic hierarchy, there can be resistance from both above and below, from within and without. That can be lonely until you find ways to connect with a new group of like-minded people and establish a new sense of belonging.

As you gain financial abundance, it may take a while until your new financial circumstances begin to feel normal and you gain a sense of confidence in your new milieu. In the meantime, be kind to yourself!

You might not have to leave behind everyone from your tribe, and I'm not saying you would *want* that. But trust me when I say that at least some of the people you know will not be able to cope if your financial circumstances radically change for the better and theirs don't. Be prepared for that, otherwise it could come as a bit of a shock.

On the other hand, when you try to enter a new social setting, it takes a while to become accustomed to the social mores of your new group. It's kind of like the transition from primary school to high school. Do you remember the anxiety that came with not fully understanding the rules of that new social environment? The process of finding your feet can be painful.

So what will you need to be successful? Well, you'll need beliefs that give you the ability to tolerate being a beginner and feeling socially awkward, while still feeling okay about yourself.

Nouveau Riche

The pressure can come from both sides of the tracks, so to speak. It's not unusual for people who are already wealthy to hold the apparent lack of social knowledge of the newly rich against them. For example, have you heard the term *nouveau riche?* It can be used as a term of disparagement by people with "old money" against those who have recently achieved wealth.

The nouveau riche are seen by those accustomed to wealth as somewhat crass, lacking in refinement, taste, and style. They're often ridiculed for their apparent need to indulge in showy displays of wealth, such as expensive cars, flashy jewelry, and the like.

But why do the newly wealthy feel the need to brashly display their financial success anyway? Perhaps they mistakenly assume that their new situation is just about money, and that they should openly show signs of wealth to prove that they have it. No display of affluence seems to be too grand for the nouveau riche.

Sadly, this is the very behavior that marks them as not truly belonging to the wealthy class in the minds of those who have grown up with such abundance. And it is the same behavior that alienates their friends who do not have as much.

The thing about the wealthy mind-set is that it is *not* just about having money; it's also about a state of mind where abundance feels completely normal. For those who have had money for a long time and who mix with others who have also had money for a long time, wealth is just a given and therefore not discussed as much as poorer people might imagine—just as gravity is an accepted state, and therefore not often mentioned. Another analogy is that when there is plenty of water around, we use it freely and don't even think much about it. It wouldn't occur to us to brag about how much water we have or to talk at length about how we use it. We just have it, and we just use it. End of story.

The thing about the wealthy mind-set is that it is *not* just about having money; it's also about a state of mind where abundance feels completely normal.

Other achievements become distinguishing traits as abundant wealth becomes an accepted state, such as knowledge of the arts, music, literature, and history. Social markers such as being well mannered, adept in the art of conversation, highly educated, and well traveled can become more important than flashy displays of wealth.

The issues I am raising here about belonging, tribal mores, and the discomforts associated with moving between social groups are not insurmountable. A solid sense of self-esteem is more than equal to the task. I raise these issues simply because they are the kind of thing that can blindside you if you're not ready for them.

Most people, no matter what they say, care a lot about what others think. Even the original desire for wealth, for some people, can be based on wanting others to think better of them—to see them as successful or smart. So it can come as a bit of a shock, especially if external approval was the deeper motivation for seeking wealth, to find out that not only do some people *not* admire them for attaining financial success, they can be downright hostile and critical toward them because of it! And this can happen in both the old and new socioeconomic class.

Compounding: The Greatest Invention of Mankind

Now that we've looked at the psychological side of the question, let's come back to the material aspects of whether it takes money to make money. What if working hard is not the best way to build wealth? What if the best method, as discussed in Chapter 4, is to break away from the *time = money* constraint and get your money working for you?

You might point out that in order to get your money working for you, you'd actually need to have some money to put to work. So, you might argue, isn't it true that it takes money to make money?

The answer, it seems, is a little bit *yes* but mostly *no*, thanks to a wonderful thing called *compounding.* You may need some investment capital to get started—some seed capital—but it doesn't necessarily have to be a huge amount thanks to the power of compounding. This allows you to escape the *time = money* constraint where you have to work hard for every dollar, and it allows you to eventually get your dollars working hard for you. Albert Einstein is said to have called compound interest "the greatest invention of mankind."

You can begin to access the power of compounding when you invest for a positive return and then take that return and invest it again. For example, if I paid you a 10 percent return per year on a $100,000 investment ($10,000 per year), and you didn't reinvest the proceeds, this would be your total return after 25 years: 25 x $10,000 = $250,000.

So after 25 years, you would have $350,000 in total capital, which is your $250,000 investment return plus your original $100,000 investment.

But if you reinvested the interest income each year so that the second year I paid you 10 percent interest on $110,000 (which is your original $100,000 investment capital plus the $10,000 in interest from the previous year that you added to your starting capital) . . . and you reinvested like this every year . . . then after 25 years, your total capital would be $1,083,471. You would have 3.1 times more capital in the end than if you hadn't reinvested. *Three* times more! That's the power of compounding.

The higher the annual return on the investment, the greater the power of compounding to boost the final result. And the longer the investment horizon, the greater the impact of compounding.

Compounding allows you to access the power of exponential growth. And the great thing about exponential growth is that it accelerates over time. Here's an example of what it looks like:

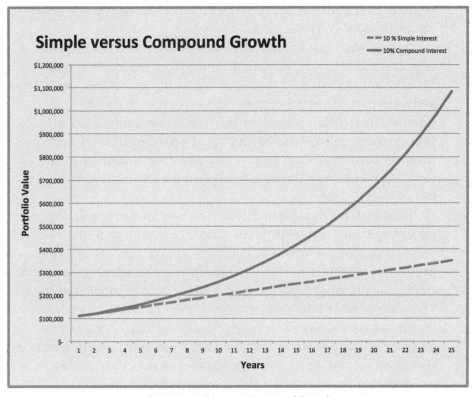

Figure 1: Simple versus Compound Growth

So while it's true that it does take some money to get started investing, the power of compounding can be your real friend when it comes to accelerating your progress over time. Years ago, I saw a great advertising campaign by an investment management firm that summed up this idea. It said: "You don't have to be wealthy to invest, but you do have to invest to be wealthy."

The key, of course, is to identify an investment strategy that will give you a decent positive rate of return or, alternatively, a good capital gain. You'll need to make informed choices about what to invest in—be it real estate, the stock market, or a great business idea. Knowledge of the risks and rewards associated with any investment is going to be essential to your success . . . unless you're very lucky, of course. But luck is not something you can replicate over and over again, whereas savvy investment acumen can be used for every decision.

It does take some knowledge to grow your wealth, and knowledge is something you may need to invest in. But don't despair! It's now easier than ever before to access the knowledge, skills, and tools to take control of your own investments, thanks to the Internet. Incredible amounts of information and numerous support systems are available at the tip of your fingers, and many investment strategies can now be executed from anywhere in the world. In many ways, there's never been a better time to take control of your financial future.

I can't advise you specifically on the best investment strategy for you to build your wealth. The strategy (or strategies) that suit you will depend on lots of things, such as your age, the amount of risk you're willing to take, how much you can afford to invest from your disposable income, and a whole host of other factors. There are plenty of different strategies that can work, depending on the market conditions. It's even possible to make money when a market is going down if you know what you're doing. The path that's best for you is going to depend on what suits your personality. It should be a path that you'll enjoy walking. Ideally, you'll love it.

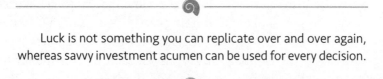

Luck is not something you can replicate over and over again, whereas savvy investment acumen can be used for every decision.

But here's the best advice I can give you: If you do have the desire to achieve financial freedom, then before you invest in knowledge, financial assets, businesses, or anything else, there is something you ought to invest in first . . .

You guessed it: a supportive set of beliefs!

Frustration, Beliefs, and Investing

Speaking from experience, the best way to avoid many long years of frustrated effort is to make sure your subconscious beliefs are in alignment with your conscious desires right from the start. Remember:

Desire + Knowledge + Belief = Success

but

Desire + Knowledge − Belief = Frustration

I know that I have reiterated this point a few times already, but the repetition is on purpose. I find that a lot of people miss this critical step, and I want to make sure that you get it so that you can avoid years of frustration.

No matter how much I focus on the importance of beliefs, I still find that people want to jump straight to the "doing" part, especially when it comes to building wealth. They want to know which strategy they should use, what the best investments are to boost their net worth quickly, whether they should have a budget, if they should invest in real estate or stocks or start their own business.

"I'm so frustrated!" they tell me. "What should I do to increase my wealth?"

The focus in this sentence is usually on the "what to do" part, when it should be on discovering what underlying belief conflicts are causing the frustration to occur in the first place.

Frustration is the key symptom here. It's a really good place to start. In fact, I've come to see frustration as a great blessing. It always shows me something important, and when I pay attention to what it's trying to teach me, then I learn something truly valuable. The dividends are huge.

So I would encourage you to resist the urge to jump to yet another frantic attempt to "do" something about your frustration, and instead just sit with it for a while and try to uncover what is driving that annoying feeling. There will always be some way in which your subconscious beliefs do not match your conscious desires whenever a lot of frustration is present. And that is a great opportunity to uncover a belief blockage and to do some reprogramming.

I know it can seem counterintuitive at first. That's because we are conditioned to believe that most solutions lie outside of ourselves. Many people want to be "seeing" before they are "believing" —in fact, they want to see in order to believe, as discussed in Chapter 2. But it just doesn't work that way.

If you don't do the belief-change work first, if you just charge ahead into implementing the next "solution," things can seem to improve for a while, but then frustration comes back just like a boomerang. The belief shift has to be accomplished first in order to banish the frustration for good.

There are plenty of ways to achieve financial freedom—ways I don't even know about, ways you don't know about, ways that haven't even been dreamed up yet. Endless roads to wealth are out there waiting for you. Endless possibilities exist. And you'll be best placed to not only see them, but also to successfully take advantage of them, once your beliefs are in alignment with your goals.

Now, let's look at where you might land if you've cleared the four money myths that we've examined so far. (You'll learn more about the how-to of clearing limiting beliefs in Chapter 10, but for now let's just imagine that you've cleared the first four myths already.)

Once you've reprogrammed yourself to believe in abundance and not scarcity, you've transcended the belief limitation of having to trade your hours for dollars or of having to always work hard for your money, you feel deserving of making money easily, and you've accessed the power of passive income streams, capital gains, and compounding to do so, then money may start to flow into your life both quickly and easily. You might think at that point that you are done: "Yay! Mission accomplished. Financial freedom here I come."

Well, watch out! There are still a few belief "trip wires" that you might encounter and that you need to be alert to.

Remember when George W. Bush announced on an aircraft carrier in 2003 that the combat in Iraq was over? He stood underneath a huge banner that said "Mission Accomplished." But then the conflict ended up grinding on unresolved for another eight years. Well, if you only clear the first four money myths and don't attend to the final three, it could wind up a bit like that for you—you could be in for many more years of frustration and conflict (of the subconscious kind).

So let's keep going. There are still more myths to bust on your journey to true financial freedom, and I want to make sure you do the job right the first time.

Digging Deep

1. If you have begun the process of moving toward greater financial freedom, have you experienced resistance from others with respect to your ideas or to actions you may have taken on this path?

2. Have you ever felt uncomfortable in a social situation because your financial circumstances were not equal to those around you—either because you had more than they did, or they had more than you did?

3. Are there any incidents you can recall where the belief that the rich get richer and the poor get poorer has affected you or played out in your life?

Action Steps

1. Think about any judgments you may have made in the past about people who have more money than

you. It doesn't have to be only those you know. This could include famous rich people such as Rupert Murdoch, Donald Trump, or even Paris Hilton. Just list any assessments you have made about them and about their characters . . . and be honest. We've all done it.

2. Look at the list you made in step 1, and ask yourself on what basis you made those judgments. Also, ask yourself whether, if you were in their shoes, you would like those judgments to be made about you. This exercise is not about right or wrong, good or bad. It's just about shifting your perspective.

3. Map out for yourself what a compounding-return scenario might look like for your personal investment capital. Apply different rates of return so that you can see for yourself how they would affect the outcome over time. Also, try adding in a portion of your current income (say 5 percent per year) to the scenario and see how that boosts the outcome, too. For example, let's say you start with $5,000 in savings and you earn $50,000 a year. And let's say the interest rate you can get on a 12-month term deposit is 2.5 percent. So, at the end of 12 months, you would have your original $5,000 in savings, plus the interest income, which would be $125. And if you saved 5 percent of your income during that year, you would have another $2,500 to add to the pile. So the next year you would be able to invest $7,625 at 2.5 percent. 12 months later, you would have that $7,625 plus the interest, which would be $190.63, plus another $2,500 that you'd saved. So in the third year you could invest $10,315.63 at 2.5 percent interest. In the fourth year, by the same calculation, your capital would grow to $13,073.52; and by the fifth year it would be $15,900.35.

4. Once you've seen what's possible from compounding returns, you'll be much more motivated to seek out methods of earning a decent rate of return. However, don't forget to also assess the risks and put in place strategies to protect your capital from significant losses. Sometimes a lower rate of return with less risk is better in the long run than seeking a higher return that comes with a greater risk of losing a significant portion of your capital. As you can see from doing step 3, compounding returns is about accelerating your progress, gaining momentum over time. Losses to your capital base can significantly set back the clock on the process.

5. Visit www.theabundancecodebook.com to access some extra content about the 7 Money Myths that I have created for you.

CHAPTER SEVEN

Money Myth #5:
Easy Come, Easy Go
"Money In, Money Out"

"Easy come, easy go" is a myth that shows its colors most dramatically in cases of sudden windfall financial gain. Why? Well, the work ethic is a kind of promise. It promises that if we follow it by working hard and not expecting too much, we will get ahead in life—just as long as we don't try to get too far ahead, too fast!

Many of us have a related underlying belief that there's no shortcut, no fast track, and no free lunch. This follows from, and works in tandem with, the beliefs that you have to work hard for your money, and that you have to have done something to justify or to be deserving of the things you receive in life.

What happens if you start to get money and success flowing into your life easily? The work-ethic beliefs can step in at that point and tell you that if you haven't worked hard, then you may not deserve it. And if you don't deserve it, then maybe you shouldn't have it.

So now you have a belief conflict: You have money that you don't really believe you deserve. The rectification for that belief conflict is to have the money flow out of your life just as quickly and easily as it came in. This situation can be summed up by the sayings "Easy come, easy go" and "Money in, money out."

This belief is not only a natural consequence of the preceding beliefs, but it can still remain even after you have cleared the first four money myths. Why? Because anything that you have heard over and over again, or possibly even repeated to yourself and others over and over again, is powerful subconscious programming code.

And that's what makes this fifth myth a particularly damaging form of sabotage, because when you have cleared the first four money myths, that is when funds are much more likely to start flowing into your life easily. There's nothing more crushing than finally attaining your heart's desire and then watching it head straight back out the door that it just came in.

You've probably heard stories of lottery winners who have gone bankrupt after a few years or have ended up with less money than before they hit the jackpot. In some cases, this has happened with winnings of hundreds of millions of dollars. How can that be? It seems extraordinary! And yet it does happen.

But surely it is a rare occurrence? Surely the incidence of such financial calamities has been inflated by our very own negativity bias? It seems not. In fact, lottery winners may actually end up being *more* likely to go bankrupt three to five years after winning than they were before they ever won the money.

A study was conducted by three economics professors, using data gathered from a list of Florida lottery winners.[1] They compared the names of winners with names in the Florida bankruptcy records to see how many of the winners had filed for bankruptcy after they won, and when.

The data showed that the bankruptcy rate among lottery winners of amounts up to $150,000 was roughly the same rate of bankruptcy as seen in the rest of the population, on average, over the five-year period after winning. That would indicate that winning the lottery did not help to reduce overall bankruptcy rate for the winners, but it also didn't increase it. However, looking at the five-year average does not tell the full story. And looking at the average across all segments of the study group doesn't quite give us the nuances either.

First let's talk about the segments. There appeared to be quite different responses depending on whether people won less than or more than $10,000. Maybe that's because an amount less than $10,000 is not likely to radically shake a person's psychological relationship with money. So I will stick to looking at the group of people who won more than $10,000.

Now let's talk about why we want to break the time period down as well. That's because what happens in the first two years after winning is radically different to what happens in the next three years.

The average bankruptcy rate for the general population in Florida during the time of the study (1993–2001) was about 1 percent per year. For the winners of $10,000 or more, this rate dipped to about 0.7 percent per year in the two years immediately after winning, but then it rocketed up to 1.3 percent per year in the following three years. So even though there was an initial dip in the bankruptcy rate for winners (as we would expect), later it not only caught up, but it got to be about one-third worse than it was before. In the end, the windfall was actually harmful to the winners' financial health!

The sample period studied ended at a horizon of five years post-win, so there is no way to know if the bankruptcy rate of the winners may have actually continued to rise beyond the horizon of the study.

Now, what about the emotional impact of winning? H. Roy Kaplan, a professor of sociology, studied lottery winners in the U.S. in the 1970s and did follow-up research in the 1980s. His work confirms the power of underlying beliefs:

> You can catapult people from one economic status to another overnight, but a lifetime of beliefs and experiences change more slowly . . . People who were outgoing and gregarious before winning took it in stride. People who were shy and withdrawn before winning became suspicious and paranoid.[2]

Kaplan appears to be saying that the preexisting underlying belief structure of the lottery winner is an important determinant of how well they will handle having a windfall gain.

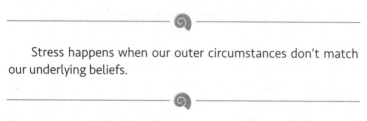

Stress happens when our outer circumstances don't match our underlying beliefs.

A similar conclusion was reached by Robert Frank, who writes a blog called *The Wealth Report* for the *Wall Street Journal*. He looked at a range of studies conducted on lottery winners in the U.S. and the U.K., and this was his take:

> Sudden wealth only exaggerates your current situation. If you're unhappy, bad with money and surrounded by people you don't trust, money will make those problems worse. If you're fulfilled, careful with money and enjoy a life of strong relationships, the lottery could make those strengths better.[3]

In other words, if you already have a supportive underlying belief structure about money, people, and life, then you will probably be able to handle suddenly acquiring wealth. But if you don't have a belief structure that supports wealth, then even if you're lucky enough to win the lottery, you may still experience subconscious sabotage that can result in emotional turmoil and financial loss. Why is that?

Perhaps it's because our brains do not like the stress of things we're not already accustomed to handling. Stress happens when our outer circumstances don't match our underlying beliefs. For most people, this occurs when something changes externally and the new situation runs counter to an inner belief. When this happens, we do things unconsciously to try to resolve our outer circumstances so that they once again match our underlying beliefs. We try to restore the subconscious equilibrium.

When money comes into your life quickly and easily, it will flow out just as quickly and easily if you have the "easy come, easy go" belief program running in the background. Usually, it happens so fast that most people don't even notice it. It may take winning the lottery or some other windfall gain to make the mechanism more obvious.

Case Study: Michael Larson

Michael Larson is famous for having won a large jackpot on the U.S. game show *Press Your Luck* in May 1984. He won the money using a system he had figured out by watching past episodes of the show.

Larson, who was mostly unemployed, had spent many hours reviewing tapes of *Press Your Luck* on his VCR and had noticed a recurring pattern in the game. In other words, he figured out a way to hack the game—a strategy that should ensure he would win if he got on the show.

He took this knowledge, and using nearly all of his savings, he made the trip to Hollywood to audition to be a contestant on the show. He was selected, and he ended up winning more than $100,000 in cash. This was unheard of on the show at that time and was a significant amount of money back in 1984. You have to hand it to him. His hack was pretty clever.

The producers of the show actually figured out that Larson had hacked the game. But they couldn't find any way that he had violated the rules, so they were forced to pay out the money he had won. They were sufficiently embarrassed by the incident, though, so they changed the patterns used in the game in a way that would prevent it being hacked again; and after the initial airings, they refused to replay the episodes of the show in which Larson appeared.

The fact that Michael Larson was able to hack *Press Your Luck* and win is pretty interesting in itself. But what happened after that is also fascinating . . . because he proceeded to lose his winnings in true "easy come, easy go" style.

First, he invested a good chunk of the cash in a real-estate investment that turned out to be a Ponzi scheme. This is essentially a scam that relies on funds from new investors all the time in order to finance the payment of returns to the earlier investors because there is no *real* underlying investment producing a positive return. When the flow of new-investor money stops, the whole thing unravels.

Do you remember Bernie Madoff? He successfully ran a Ponzi scheme in the U.S. for what many estimate to have been more than 30 years—one of the largest frauds in U.S. history. It unraveled in 2008 after the global financial crisis began, presumably when the supply of new-investor funds dried up. That scheme defrauded investors of many billions of dollars. Madoff was convicted of fraud and sentenced to 150 years of jail time.

So, coming back to the Michael Larson story, Larson invested a bunch of his winnings in something that turned out to be a Ponzi scheme, and he ended up losing all of that money very quickly.

Next, he heard about a competition on the radio where the person who had a dollar bill with a particular serial number on it would be paid $30,000 if they were able to produce the bill. So Larson started withdrawing his remaining winnings from the bank in $1 notes, and then he and his wife spent hours checking the serial numbers on the bills, trying to find one that matched the serial number that had been announced on the radio. This was pretty tiring work.

After checking the serial numbers on 40,000 bills (or $40,000 worth, which represented most of what he had left from his game-show winnings), Larson and his wife decided they needed a break. They went out to a Christmas party, leaving the bills stuffed in bags at home. While they were out, their place got robbed, and the entire $40,000 was stolen!

Trading Psychology

Lottery winners have been studied a lot, and that research is certainly very interesting, but what other group of people frequently comes up against the "easy come, easy go" myth?

For traders, the "easy come, easy go" belief can be in play when they are inclined toward excessive risk taking.

Speaking from my own personal and professional experience, I can say that financial market traders, as a group, do battle with their underlying psychology on a daily basis. So I'm going to spend a bit of time talking about trading psychology because it's relevant to the discussion, and I do happen to have a lot of personal experience with it.

For traders, the "easy come, easy go" belief can be in play when they are inclined toward excessive risk taking. When a trader takes large risks—even if they're calculated, "rational" risks that are being entered into for logical reasons—it's usually only because there's a large potential payoff. That is *easy come*. And this is usually accompanied by the risk of a large potential loss. That is *easy go*.

Successful traders manage the downside risks well, are able to short-circuit their fear response when markets are volatile and going against them, and learn how to avoid getting caught up in the euphoria that can trigger a greed response when things are going their way.

Mastering the Emotions of Fear and Greed

Traders often comment that trading the financial markets is 10 percent about trading strategy and 90 percent about psychology. They talk a lot about the twin psychological nemeses of trading:

fear and greed. It can take years for traders to truly master their own psychology and become seasoned, levelheaded professionals.

It's been my personal theory that often the problem lies with the "easy come, easy go" belief. When you think about it, the greed for gain aspect in trading is lust for the *easy come* part of this particular myth, while fear of loss is anxiety about the *easy go* part. (It turns out that basic physiology plays a part, too. I'll explain the research behind that a little later, and why it gels with my own experience.)

I noticed when I spent some years working in the funds-management division at a major Australian merchant bank that it is often older men and women who end up being the best traders. They are somehow better able to keep a cool head.

The young male traders were the ones whose trading accounts tended to have trading profits and losses (P&L) that swung all over the place. Sure, when they had a good year, they had a great year. The problem was that when that happened, they got rewarded with huge bonuses, which reinforced the risk-taking behavior. But eventually (perhaps inevitably) the reckoning would come. And when it did, it could be messy. I worked there during the dot-com boom and bust years, so I saw how the traders responded to some pretty crazy market conditions.

As I mentioned, I noticed that the traders who did well over the longer haul, and across both boom and bust conditions, were the older traders.

Case Study: Nancy

In the bank that I worked at, the highest paid trader was a woman I'll call Nancy. Her trading track record was incredibly consistent and profitable year after year. This had gained the bank more than a billion dollars in funds under management for the product she managed. That's probably because consistency is a lot easier to sell than a wildly variable P&L, where the potential for high returns comes with the potential for large losses as well.

As I watched Nancy and her consistent success, I became intrigued. I began to study her behavior compared to that of her male counterparts. I noticed that the men, especially the younger men, had a tendency to get "married" to their view. They seemed to have a need to be right. And they often held on to their positions for too long.

Perhaps, I guessed, they were overly attached to believing they were right, and they resisted admitting they could be wrong. Despite much evidence that they were probably wrong when things were going against them, they doggedly held the view that the market would eventually turn around and validate them, proving that they were right after all.

Nancy was different. Instead of getting married to her view and failing to cut her losses when things went against her, I noticed that Nancy seemed to *assume* she might be wrong from the start.

I noticed that as soon as Nancy placed a trade, she immediately began the process of asking what early warning signs would indicate that she was, in fact, wrong. She seemed to look for these contrary signs as vigilantly as she looked for confirming signs that might indicate her view was correct. Nancy would also actively push the market analysts working there (like myself) to consider what economic or market developments would indicate that she might be wrong, and she would thereby be instructing us to keep our eyes open to such signs and to alert her if we saw them.

In contrast, the guys generally seemed to want to know more about things that confirmed their existing view regarding a trade, rather than things that might contradict it. In this way, Nancy came at it from a totally different angle to the men.

Now, Nancy's way of thinking didn't stop her from taking a strong view and backing that view in the first place. She had the courage of her convictions to take an informed, rational bet and get in the game with a good chance of being right. That exposed her to the upside potential. But I feel that Nancy's different mindset meant that she usually saw the writing on the wall when things turned against her a bit earlier than the guys did. I think that helped her in limiting her downside because she was more able to get out fast enough to prevent large losses from accumulating in her trading account.

I also noticed that on the upside, when things did go well for her, Nancy was grateful and remained humble about it. Even when she did turn out to be right, she didn't "big-note" herself. She seemed to realize that it could have turned out differently—she easily might not have been right because it was a bit of a numbers game.

So Nancy didn't get a big head about it, and she took her profits appropriately. She closed out when it became evident that her run had probably come to an end. And she didn't seem to worry about this occasionally meaning that her profits were not as great as they could have been if she'd held on a bit longer.

The young guys, on the other hand, often hung on to their positions for too long even when they were right (perhaps getting caught up in greed, or wanting to be even *more* right?) and then watched as the market turned around and took back most, or all, of their previous gains. And when they did close out early, if the trade then continued to run in a profitable direction, it seemed to cause them a *lot* of pain. They hated watching the one that got away.

Why was Nancy apparently—according to my subjective observations—so much more levelheaded in her trading than the younger guys?

Maybe I'm being too hard on them. Is this sounding like the gender opposite of the old propaganda that used to assert that women are not suited for the same kinds of roles as men—such as being able to make informed decisions about politics and vote accordingly or having the aptitude to study science, mathematics, or engineering?

I certainly don't want to mount those kinds of flawed arguments (in reverse), and I want to be very careful about not making broad generalizations from my own very limited experience. Especially when I wholeheartedly acknowledge that I am as vulnerable as the next person to confirmation bias. So let's look at some data.

The Biology of Trading

Recent scientific research on the biology of traders suggests that basic human physiology and chemistry could have been part of the secret to Nancy's success. It turns out that the higher the level of testosterone in the body, the more risk traders are inclined to take on.

For 12 years, John Coates was a derivatives trader with Goldman Sachs, Merrill Lynch, and Deutsche Bank. He observed first-hand the way that traders can get caught up in a bubble, a market frenzy fueled by greed and "irrational exuberance." And on the flip side, he saw the way fear can suddenly grip both traders and the broader market, causing a crash.

Is this the "easy come, easy go" belief being acted out in a broader market sense? I have often wondered if market bubbles and crashes are somehow created by the underlying group psychology of market participants or if they are more a consequence of our cognitive biases, driven by our evolutionary neuronal conditioning, or both.

I guess John Coates wondered about that, too. While he was still a trader, Coates became fascinated with advances in neuroscience, and he couldn't help wondering what was going on chemically in the bodies and brains of his fellow traders. In the end, he decided to find out.

Coates wanted to know how the level of hormone and chemicals in the body changed in response to market conditions, and how that might be linked to observed trading behavior.

Coates retired as a trader to study neuroscience and endocrinology at the University of Cambridge, and he continued his work there as a senior research fellow. As described on his website:

He suspected that the waves of irrational exuberance and pessimism de-stabilizing the financial markets may be driven by physiological changes taking place within traders as they make or lose money and as market volatility rises and falls.[4]

Coates went back to the trading floor after he completed his studies and started testing the saliva of traders while they were engaged in trading and experiencing market ups and downs. He conducted experiments on 250 professional traders in the City, London's financial district. The tests allowed him to measure the levels of various hormones, such as testosterone and the stress hormone cortisol. He presents the full results of his research in his acclaimed book *The Hour Between Dog and Wolf.*

Coates wanted to know how the level of hormones and chemicals in the body changed in response to market conditions, and how that might be linked to observed trading behavior. His tests led him to conclude that a higher level of testosterone in the body leads to more excessive risk-taking behavior. Of course, higher testosterone levels are more prevalent in younger males.

In the wake of the global financial crisis and the subsequent volatility in financial markets, what is John Coates's prescription for reducing the risk of bubbles (excessive booms) and crashes (excessive busts) in financial markets? Add more female and older male traders to the trading floors!

"Women have about 10 percent to 20 percent of the testosterone found in males," says Coates, according to a Bloomberg News report on his research, "while levels of the hormone in men decline as they mature."[5]

It's a bit of a radical idea. I wonder if it will ever happen. It could be achieved by changing the recruitment criteria for traders in major investment banks, proprietary trading desks, and asset-management firms—that is, actually take steps through different hiring policies to change the biology of the financial markets. The problem is, this sounds kind of discriminatory. I doubt that the human resources departments of the major banks are going to rush to implement it. How would you like to be told, "I'm sorry, you're just not biologically suited for this job."

I actually think that this research highlights why habits are sometimes a very important overlay to any belief-change work. I'll talk more about this in Chapter 10. Basically, if it is about more than just beliefs—if you are also sometimes battling your own physiology in order to make good decisions—then a good set of habits can be very important.

Sticking to the Plan

Say you want to trade and invest in financial markets, yet you happen to be a young man who is naturally filled with apparently judgment-impairing levels of testosterone, or you are in the grip of the "easy come, easy go" belief. What could you do?

First, I would recommend dealing with the limiting belief issue. However, if physiology and hormonal influences are also a potential factor, then it's a good idea to be aware of it and take steps to prevent them from having a negative impact on your investment decisions. For that purpose, you could find yourself an older male trading or investing mentor. You also could consider running your investment strategies past a woman who is also suitably knowledgeable. Or you could just recognize that you may be vulnerable to physiologically driven instances of poor judgment and take steps to make sure you practice discipline.

Make some rules for yourself, and set up some helpful habits. This is a good idea even if you're *not* in the grip of your hormones. For example, you could construct an investment plan while you are not in the heat of the moment, when you aren't caught up in your emotions or vulnerable to physiologically impaired judgments, and commit to sticking to that plan.

Trading and investing can be exciting and stimulating. But this can quickly cross the line into hyperstimulation, stress, and anxiety. Having a clear plan and sticking to it can really help to manage stress levels and help you avoid making bad decisions.

Discipline can overcome a lot. But be aware that your brain chemistry can have a powerful influence on your decision making. There are other hormones apart from testosterone that affect your ability to make rational decisions, like serotonin. Low levels of this hormone can impair impulse control. People with low serotonin have trouble stopping themselves from taking actions that have not been carefully thought through. In other words, low serotonin can make it more difficult to stick to the plan.

Stress, not enough sleep, poor diet, certain chemical addictions like caffeine and sugar, insufficient protein or complex carbohydrates, lack of exercise, life dramas, not getting enough sunshine to the light cones in your eyes . . . all of these things can have a detrimental impact on your brain's serotonin production. So simple healthy habits like eating well, having a regular sleep schedule, exercising, and getting outside in the sun from time to time can help you to make better decisions. That applies to all areas of life, not just money matters.

If sticking to the plan doesn't work, then taking a break can be a really good alternative. If you're feeling a bit down, low in energy, or off your game, it could be a signal that it's time to take a break—and to avoid making any big decisions about your investments.

I know someone who loves to day-trade. That means he watches every little movement in the market all day long and enters and exits multiple positions each day. He knows what he's doing, he has a trading system (a plan), and he generally makes quite well-informed and rational decisions that have a good chance of being profitable. But he also knows that he can't sustain the kind of focused attention and discipline that day-trading requires for too long at a stretch.

He noticed a pattern in his trading over time: If he tried to keep day-trading for more than a few weeks without taking a break, he started making poor decisions and was soon giving up all the gains he had spent the prior weeks or months carefully accumulating in his account.

So he made a rule for himself: He now only day-trades for a maximum of three weeks at a time, and then he takes a break for at least a week. He finds that this rhythm keeps him fresh and coolheaded, and that as a result he is less likely to make ill-advised, emotionally driven decisions in his trading.

Am I "Easy Come, Easy Go"?

Even though it may be pretty unlikely that you'll win the lottery or hack your way to win a lot of money on a game show, and even though you may not have actually experienced the roller coaster of emotions that can come with trading financial markets, you may still have the "easy come, easy go" program running your subconscious mind. But how would you know? This one can be pretty subtle for a lot of people.

In fact, the "easy come, easy go" belief will often only surface once you've already tackled some of the other subconscious barriers to wealth—like the belief that you have to work hard for your money or that time is money—the kinds of codes that limit your ability to generate wealth quickly. What I mean is that until you've tackled those other limiting beliefs, you're unlikely to actually experience the *easy come* part of the equation.

But take a moment to think back over your life . . . have you had any experiences where there's been a sudden, unexpected influx of money? Have you ever received an inheritance? Have you ever had a big win betting on the races, at the casino, or on poker machines?

What happened? Did that money stay in your life for long? Or did you spend it, distribute it, or otherwise consume it right away? Did you invest any of the funds in a way that would help you make more money in the future?

Also think about your family and how they may have behaved in similar circumstances, because it's pretty likely that you've inherited some subconscious programming from them. If your parents ever got a financial windfall or inheritance, for example, how long did the money last? Did they invest it? Or did they spend it on holidays, or perhaps cars, jewelry, or things that were fairly transitory and unlikely to provide an income stream or be worth more in the future?

The "easy come, easy go" belief will often only surface once you've already tackled some of the other subconscious barriers to wealth.

Answering questions like these may help you to recognize whether or not you might have the "easy come, easy go" program running in the background of your subconscious mind. I know I did, and it took me a long time (and many financial ups and downs) before I finally realized that I was very much in the grip of this myth . . . and also the myth that money wouldn't make me happy, which I will discuss in the next chapter.

Digging Deep

1. Have you ever experienced a sudden windfall? If so, how long did the money last, and how did you use it? How much of that money did you spend, and how much, if any, did you invest?

2. Can you think of any situations where you have seen the "easy come, easy go" belief in action, either in yourself or in someone you know? Describe what happened.

3. If you are actively trading or investing, have you ever noticed yourself doing battle with the emotions of fear and greed?

Action Steps

1. Notice when money comes into your life easily and stop, take a breath, and think before you take any steps that might make it all slip away just as easily. Ask yourself why you're inclined to allow the money to flow out of your life. Do you feel like you don't deserve it? What's going on at a deeper level? Just ask yourself some questions about this. Then ask yourself if, instead of spending it all, you could put some of it to work to make you more money in the future.

2. When you experience strong emotions like fear or greed with respect to your money, again just stop, take a breath, and ask yourself if what you are about to do is in line with your plan. If it doesn't align with your plan, ask yourself why you want to do it. (Oh, and if you don't have a plan for growing your wealth, make one. Even if it's just saving and investing for compound interest as discussed in Chapter 6.)

3. When it comes to big decisions about your money or your investments, ask yourself if you're in the right state of mind to be making those important decisions. Are you tired, stressed, or feeling overly anxious? If you're not in a good frame of mind, take the time to ask a trusted friend or mentor (who is not in a similarly compromised state of mind) for some advice.

4. Visit www.theabundancecodebook.com to access some extra content about the 7 Money Myths that I have created for you.

Money Myth #6: Money Won't Make You Happy
"There's More to Life Than Money"

In this myth we have another commonly held notion: Money can't buy happiness, love, or anything of true meaning or value in life. The idea is summed up in the following sayings:

- "There's more to life than money."
- "Money can't buy you happiness."
- "Money can't buy you love."
- "More money, more problems."

Let's say we just take the first of these sayings at face value and accept that there is more to life than money. It's hard to argue with that, because obviously there are many experiences that have a depth of meaning and importance that cannot be accessed purely by trying to buy them. These include experiences such as falling in love, watching your children take their first steps, and spontaneous laughter and joy.

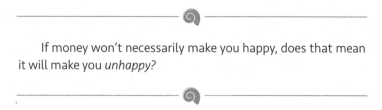

If money won't necessarily make you happy, does that mean it will make you unhappy?

But what I want to examine here is the complex equivalence (or nonequivalence) of money and happiness. If money won't necessarily make you happy, does that mean it will make you *unhappy?* Are there circumstances in which money can help facilitate happiness? If so, in what ways can having money support or assist your pursuit of happiness?

What Does the Research Say?

Elizabeth Dunn is a researcher at the University of British Columbia in Canada. She has completed a number of studies on the relationship between money and happiness. In fact, you could say she's a little bit obsessed with the topic. In one study that Dunn conducted with her colleague Lara Aknin and Michael Norton of Harvard Business School, people were asked to predict the happiness levels of others. It turns out that the test subjects expected people with low incomes to be less happy than they actually were.[1]

Why? One possibility is that there could be non-monetary benefits. If some people have actually chosen to have a lower income because they wish to have more time to do other things they enjoy, then this may give them a better perceived quality of life than we would typically expect by purely looking at their income. The value they place on the additional time has to be factored in.

However, another influence may be at play. Remember the study mentioned in the discussion of Myth #4 from researchers at the University of New South Wales in Australia? It found that children from low-income families adapted their preferences away from things they knew they couldn't have due to lack of money, just so that they could avoid the feelings that come from deprivation.[2] This kind of effect could help explain why those on lower incomes reported better happiness levels than others had expected they would—because they had already adapted their preferences as a mental compensation.

Coming back to the question of money and happiness, there are other studies that indicate there *is* a strong correlation between income and happiness. For example, according to research conducted in the U.S. by the Pew Research Center, incomes were strongly correlated with self-reported happiness levels—the higher the income, the higher the subjective happiness rating.[3] Dunn's own research on subjective happiness ratings and income levels produced a similar finding.

So . . . *does* money actually make us happier? Well, it seems that it might. But it's also fair to say that this point has long been a source of contention among economic researchers.

The Easterlin Paradox

The backstory to the debate is well described in a *New York Times* article published in 2008.[4] The conundrum arose out of research that was conducted in Japan in the post-WWII years (when Japan's wealth increased rapidly), which indicated that the Japanese people's subjective happiness had actually declined over the same period. Some findings in a few other countries seemed to agree with this trend. The fact that higher incomes in some countries were not always accompanied by greater happiness ratings became known as the "Easterlin Paradox," named after Richard Easterlin, the economist who first described it.

However, a closer examination of the data that was collected in Japan has since shown that the survey questions had actually changed over time in a way that may have accounted for the somewhat counterintuitive result originally reported. Furthermore, an examination of a wide cross section of United Nations data indicates that, broadly speaking, there does appear to be a positive correlation between national income and reported happiness levels across most countries.[5]

At this point, a statistician would jump in and tell you that correlation does not equal causation.

An examination of a wide cross section of United Nations data indicates that, broadly speaking, there does appear to be a positive correlation between national income and reported happiness levels across most countries.

In other words, just because higher happiness levels and higher income levels tend to go together, higher income does not necessarily *cause* higher happiness. There might be no actual causal relationship (known as *spurious correlation*), or causation could flow the other way around: It could be that happiness causes higher incomes.

How would that work? Well, perhaps a positive outlook and mind-set could give people the courage to stretch and grow, and a consequence of that could be that those people might tend to gain more skills and earn more money. It could be a case of "Which came first, the chicken or the egg?"

The upshot is that the causal relationship between money and happiness may be a complex one, but in a broad aggregate sense we can say with a reasonable degree of certainty that they do tend to go together.

The Generosity Effect: How Giving Makes You Happier

Elizabeth Dunn—the researcher from Canada whose work focuses on money and happiness—may have found an ingenious solution to ensure that more money does serve to improve our happiness. The answer is to spread some of the bounty around.

Another study Dunn conducted in conjunction with Lara Aknin of the University of British Columbia and Michael Norton of Harvard Business School showed that spending as little as $5 a day on someone else can significantly boost happiness.[6]

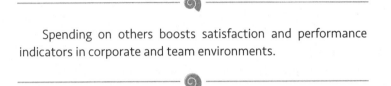

Spending on others boosts satisfaction and performance indicators in corporate and team environments.

They tested this hypothesis in Canada and in Uganda in order to rule out any specific cultural effects. That is, they chose cultural settings that were worlds apart so to speak.

Although the way in which people spent the money on others differed greatly between the two countries (someone in Canada might choose to buy roses for their mother, for example, while someone in Uganda might be more inclined to buy medicine to ease a friend's pain) the effect on reported happiness levels was remarkably similar.

They also found that spending on others boosts satisfaction and performance indicators in corporate and team environments. In one test, employees in a large Australian bank were given money to spend on charitable projects through a program called Karma Currency.[7] This action significantly boosted their reported job satisfaction levels compared to a control group who spent the money on themselves.

In another test, teams were given money to either spend on themselves or to spend on their teammates. The researchers tested two very different groups, again in order to ensure the results were robust and not due to some random cultural factor: Belgian pharmaceutical sales teams and Canadian dodgeball teams.

The results? The Belgian pharmaceutical teams whose members spent the money on their teammates outsold the teams where members spent the money on themselves. And the Canadian dodgeball teams whose members spent the money on their teammates won more games than teams where members had spent the money on themselves.

Let's Apply Some Common Sense

Money can make the practicalities of life a lot easier. Money can help make life less stressful. Money can mean that you don't have to worry about having enough to get the essentials for survival. On the flip side, *not* having enough money for food, shelter, and clothing for you and your family members can be really stressful. Even the fear of one day not having enough can cause anxiety.

My favorite saying on the topic is, "Money might not buy you happiness, but it makes a darn good down payment!" But in order to short-circuit the desire for abundant wealth, many of us fall back on this old nugget: "There's more to life than money."

Okay, yes there is. But what we often do not sufficiently acknowledge are the negative consequences of not having financial freedom:

- Not having enough money can be a huge source of stress for us and our families.

- Even people who appear to be affluent can suffer from financial stress if they have accessed their lifestyle through a high reliance on debt.

- The need to exchange most of our time for money often keeps us away from our family members and friends and prevents us from doing the things we love.

- Not having a good work-life balance can threaten our health, our longevity, and our feeling of vitality because working long hours is tiring and physically draining.

Yet we can't deny that there exists a type of stress that comes with always striving for more and more. Everyone wants enough money to cover the essentials of life. But just having what we need for survival doesn't seem to be enough for many of us. A lot of people want to look after their needs beyond just the basics.

A Catch-22 Situation

This is the paradox: We find ourselves trapped in a loop of having to work harder and harder in order to get what we want so that we can have a better quality of life, but we actually end up sacrificing our quality of life in the process. For example, we want to be able to have nice food, nice shelter, and nice clothes . . . and a good car . . . and a cool stereo . . . and a big-screen TV . . . and good schools for our children . . . and the list goes on. If we're still stuck in the old belief paradigm, we have to work harder to get more money to be able to afford these things.

If we are still rooted in the belief structure that says we have to work hard for our money, then wanting more money will lead us down a path of working harder and having less time.

Many of us then find ourselves wanting even more: the latest car, the coolest stereo, the best home-theater system, the most prestigious schools for our children. Why? Because having more money and better stuff than our peers, it turns out, is also something that correlates strongly with being happier.[8]

So we work even harder to make more money in order to have better stuff than our neighbors . . . and then what? We see less of our children, spend less time in our nice house, have less fun, and forget to make time for self-reflection. This can lead to feeling stressed, unhealthy, and miserable.

It's a bit of a Catch-22 situation, because now we can't stop. We have to keep going to pay the mortgage, the car loan, the credit-card bills, and the school fees! What a bind. What to do? Well, paradoxically, many people decide to work even harder in order to make more money to fix the problem!

It's natural to want more money. Yet it's easy to see where the belief that money won't buy happiness has come from. Because if we are still rooted in the belief structure that says we have to work hard for our money and that we have to exchange more of our precious, limited time if we want more money, then wanting more money will lead us down a path of working harder and having less time. That's not usually a happy place to end up!

As it turns out, this happiness thing is a bit of a juggling act. It seems possible that a single-minded focus on having more money (rather than more freedom, more choices, or the ability to access a broader range of experiences) can actually impair a person's ability to enjoy life. While it's true that greater wealth *can* improve happiness levels, working harder and harder in order to have more money can undo the positive effects gained from increasing income.

The Pew Research Center study showed that good health has an even stronger correlation with happiness than money does, and if we work too hard, we tend to sacrifice our health. Another major driver of happiness, the study revealed, is being in a strong relationship or being married. Our relationships can come under a lot of stress if we're working really long hours, which can lead to breakups and emotional suffering.

In a way it's a trap we have set for ourselves—or rather, it's a trap that our own limiting beliefs have set for us. We work hard (because we believe we have to) in order to get the things that we think will make us happy, and in the process we can end up making ourselves tired and miserable.

The Rat Race

Isn't one definition of insanity doing the same thing over and over, yet expecting a different outcome? One particular brand of insanity, in my opinion, is called the rat race. You know you're in the rat race when the following are true:

- You don't love what you do, but you feel you have to do it anyway.
- You work overly long hours and lack balance in your life.
- You're tired and unfulfilled.
- It's hard to get out of bed and go to work in the morning.
- You wish you had more time to see your family and friends.
- You dream about holidays, yet rarely allow yourself to take them.
- You know your health is suffering as you sit in your air-conditioned office, huddled in your cubicle, staring at your computer screen, and squinting under the harsh fluorescent lights.
- You avoid thinking about how long you will have to do this.

So why do it? Usually, we do it for money—or at least for the things that money can buy. But if we have to work 50 to 80 hours a week, hardly ever see our family and friends, and run ourselves down physically in the process, is that a good outcome?

Not really. It's not an outcome that is likely to lead to happiness for most people.

What's the Why?

Our motivation may be an important factor in determining whether or not money will help us to be happy. For example, if we want more money in order to "win" or to be "better" than others, then wealth probably won't make us happy. There will always be someone else who has a nicer house, a hotter partner, a bigger yacht, or whatever other external evidence of being better we have set our minds on.

But if our goal is to have more choices, to be in a position to be more generous and abundant, to be free to follow our heart's desire, to have great experiences, to grow, to live life to the fullest, then money can certainly help with that. Once again, the underlying belief structure is very important. Are our actions based on a belief in scarcity and competition or a belief in abundance and generosity? The belief is what drives the motivation.

If our motivation is to be better than others because we've gained more wealth, power, or status—well, this kind of motivation stems from an inner belief that we are somehow not good enough the way we are. But if the motivation is about having freedom, choices, and abundance because we want to get the best out of life—that kind of motivation stems from a belief that says we are inherently worthy and deserving of having a good life.

If our goal is to have more choices, to be in a position to be more generous and abundant, to be free to follow our heart's desire, to grow, to live life to the fullest, then money can certainly help with that.

It's probably important at this stage to accept that money is not going to be able to satisfy all of our needs. There's a lot more to the fulfillment of our broader human needs than "stuff" could ever provide. Nonetheless, what about a lack of money, freedom, or choices in life? As we've been examining, aren't those things that may actually cause us to be unhappy?

For example, according to psychologist Abraham Maslow's classic hierarchy of needs (Figure 2, below), it is going to be difficult for us to be happy if our basic needs for food, shelter, and safety aren't being met.[9] Happiness is perhaps kind of a luxury in that sense. If our basic physiological needs are not being met, we're probably going to be miserable.

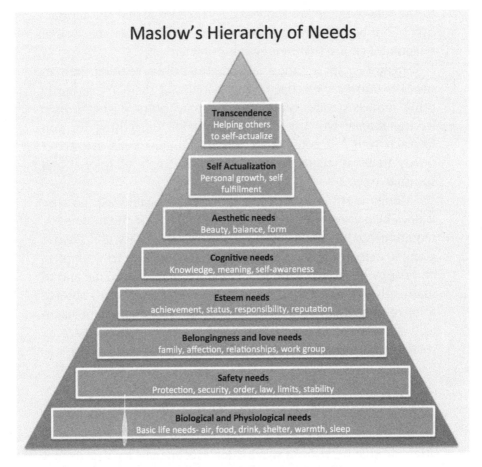

Figure 2: Maslow's Hierarchy of Needs Model

It's a journey of evolution to realize one's full potential as characterized by the higher stages of self-actualization and transcendence in Maslow's model. But reaching this kind of evolved stage can be difficult to achieve if our other more basic needs are not being met—that's why Maslow saw it as a hierarchy.

Once you have enough to eat, for example, then you can start to worry about safety. But if you're starving, you might be willing to do some pretty risky things in order to get food. Once you have the safety issue sorted, you might be able to turn your attention to fulfilling your need for affection, and so on. So bringing this back to the role of money in modern life, the fact is that the satisfaction of our basic human needs is easier when we have the kind of freedom of choice that money can provide.

Spending a lot of time analyzing the full range of our human needs is outside the scope of this book, and there are certainly other models besides Maslow's. My main point is that simply having money will not magically provide everything for you to reach your full potential. There are human needs that aren't purely material; there are some that have more emotional and spiritual aspects.

Money is still very important, as we've established, because it does help a lot when it comes to providing for the more basic requirements like clothing, food, shelter, and safety. But it's not going to meet the full range of needs that contribute to a complete and happy life. That's kind of an obvious statement to me and to many others. I'm emphasizing it, however, because I still observe a lot of people acting as if they believe that money will magically solve all of their problems. And when they finally become wealthy, it can come as a bit of shock to find out that it doesn't.

Case Study: Living the Dream

A somewhat unexpected problem can arise when we actually attain all that we've been striving for. Most people have goals that they are working toward in life, and most of the time the goals require money. As long as we don't have enough funds to achieve all of our goals right now, then "the good life" resides in the future. That means we have a convenient way of explaining why we might not be experiencing an ideal level of happiness today.

But what happens when we finally get enough money to achieve the goals and live out the dreams we set for ourselves? Well, it can be a devastating event for some people because if they are *still* not happy . . . how can they explain that?

In his book *Happier,* author and former Harvard lecturer Tal Ben-Shahar describes the problem:

> Many of us have limitations that are self-generated. When we do not feel that we are worthy of happiness, we cannot possibly feel worthy of the good things in our lives, the things that bring us happiness. Because we do not believe we actually deserve them, that they could really be ours, we fear their loss. This fear causes actual behaviors that lead to a self-fulfilling prophecy: our fear of loss creates actual loss; our feelings of being unworthy of happiness in fact lead to unhappiness.[10]

I think that might be exactly what happened to my parents . . . My parents had managed to achieve most of their life goals and dreams by the age of 40. They had both attained a high standard of education. My father in a wonderful career as a highly respected surgeon, as well as being a high-ranking officer in the Army Reserve, while my mother, who had previously been a nurse, was pursuing her intellectual interests by studying for a degree in philosophy.

They'd made some very smart investments and had attained a level of wealth that allowed them many choices in life. As I described in Chapter 1, they'd built their dream home on the shores of a picturesque lake. They had fulfilling hobbies and shared interests, which included getting their pilot's licenses and flying their own airplanes, collecting art, traveling, skiing, and playing golf. They had a wide group of social connections, and they loved giving fantastic parties.

To cap it all off, they had three children who were high achievers, both academically and in their chosen sports. Life was pretty fabulous. There seemed little else for them to attain, except maybe more of the same.

And yet . . . they weren't happy. Furthermore, they no longer had a ready excuse for that fact.

Within a few years of attaining the height of their wealth and dreams, they'd thrown it all away and were divorced, depressed, and virtually penniless.

While the realization of their dreams had remained in the future, they could rationalize why they weren't happy. Perhaps they thought that happiness might come when they got everything else that they wanted. *Then* they could relax and be happy. But when they had already achieved all of their desires, and they still weren't happy—well, that may have triggered a psychological crisis of sorts. Maybe that's why they began to drink . . . and drink . . . and drink some more . . . until all that they'd achieved slowly slid away into the ridiculous and dramatic blur that their lives (and ours, as their children) became.

Within a few years of attaining the height of their wealth and dreams, they'd thrown it all away and were divorced, depressed, and virtually penniless.

Eventually my parents were able, separately, to rebuild their lives from the rubble—to some extent, that is. Neither of them was able to re-create a significant level of wealth. In fact, they seemed to me to be somewhat scared of the prospect, and I felt I could detect in each of them behavior designed to actively avoid the possibility of attaining real financial freedom ever again.

It was many years before I realized how I, as one of their children, had coded those events in my own subconscious mind. I'd installed a core belief that I could either be happy and content in life, or I could be wealthy—but not both. I'd also installed a version of the "easy come, easy go" belief about money.

Consequently, when I became an adult, as my fortunes would rise, my life would begin to unravel. And as my fortunes would fall, I would actually begin to feel better—despite the discomfort of having a more limited range of choices available to me. Yet consciously at least, I still wanted wealth and financial freedom. I was still striving for it outwardly.

After the roller-coaster ride of financial ups and downs I described earlier in the book, I eventually recognized this. I identified many other limiting beliefs that I was harboring, and I started working to change my subconscious programming.

I now feel that I am able to experience both wealth *and* contentment without generating a subconscious conflict. Now money can come into my life easily, my wealth can continue to grow, and I don't have to manufacture circumstances wherein I experience unhappiness or discontent just because I happen to have wealth.

Still, one of the lessons I learned from my family's experience is that it's possible to have expectations about money and wealth that are unrealistic. Just having money will not solve all of life's problems. If we have emotional challenges—unresolved childhood traumas, issues with family, or difficulty forming and sustaining healthy relationships—money is not going to magically solve those problems for us. We still have to do the healing work required to deal with our emotional baggage so that we can live a happier life.

However, if you are able to create wealth and free yourself from the rat race, money can provide you with the time, the resources, and the energy to establish a life in which the broad range of your human needs could be met. In other words . . . having money can really help!

If we have money and we have time, then we also have the freedom and space needed to be able to start addressing any emotional issues we may be carrying—and that can definitely lead to greater happiness. Money may not be a panacea, but I believe it can certainly be used to facilitate an increase in happiness and well-being. That's been my experience, anyway. However, it's not lost on me that this is precisely because it's what I believe!

Digging Deep

1. What is your experience of the relationship between money and happiness?

2. Do you think that being stressed about money reduces your ability to enjoy life and be happy?

3. Do you believe that money would allow you to access a greater level of happiness? If so, how? What are your expectations about how more money would influence your happiness?

Action Steps

1. Think of the times in your life when you have been happiest. These experiences may or may not have had much to do with money . . . just note whether they did or didn't. Make a list of the happiest experiences you have had in your life. Is there a theme?

2. Similarly, make a list of the unhappiest times in your life. Is there a theme?

3. If there is a theme to your happiness, think about how money might allow you to make choices that would support more of that kind of experience. Write these choices down.

4. If there is a theme to your unhappiness, think about how money could allow you to make choices that would lessen the impact of that kind of experience on your life. Write these choices down.

5. Take the list of choices from steps 3 and 4, and use them to make affirmation and intention statements written in the present tense. For example, if you feel that money would allow you to spend more time

with your family, and this would make you happier, then your aspiration statement might be something like *I have financial security and freedom, and I choose to spend more time with my family, doing things we love to do together.* If you feel that money would allow you to be able to spend a couple of weeks a year at a health retreat, and you feel that this would lower your stress and anxiety levels, your aspiration statement might be something like *I have financial security and freedom, and I choose to care for myself by spending one week every six months relaxing and rejuvenating at a health retreat of my choice.* Don't worry if these things are still in the future for you. It's important to state them in the present tense. We'll do more with affirmations in the final chapter, so this is just a warm-up exercise.

6. Visit www.theabundancecodebook.com to access some extra content about the 7 Money Myths that I have created for you.

CHAPTER NINE

Money Myth #7:
Money Corrupts You
"Money Is the Root of All Evil"

In this final myth we have a very disturbing idea: that having money will somehow turn you from a good person into a bad one. It will corrupt you. A related myth is that if you have a strong desire to have money, then that must mean that you are, and maybe always have been, a bad or selfish person at heart. This is summed up by the saying, "Money is the root of all evil." The thinking goes kind of like this:

- If you do manage to overcome the practical, psychological, and subconscious barriers to becoming wealthy, then rather than experiencing a life of abundance, freedom, and choice, the reward will instead be that you somehow mysteriously turn into a hard-hearted, moneygrubbing miser.

- You will (for some reason) lose all sense of compassion, social responsibility, and largesse toward those who are less fortunate than yourself, and become kind of like the character of Ebenezer Scrooge in Charles Dickens's *A Christmas Carol*.

- Because of this evil transformation of your character—which, the myth implies, naturally accompanies the acquisition of wealth and money— you will very likely go to hell.

- At any rate, you probably won't get into heaven . . .

This is pretty heavy stuff! Should you believe that if you attain abundant wealth, it means you're *not* going to heaven? For a lot of people—especially those who believe that heaven is the ultimate destination of a well-lived life—that's the worst possible penalty. And it represents a *huge* incentive to remain financially constrained.

Because the Bible Tells Us So

Here is the actual quote from the Bible that formed the basis of this myth, based on more recent and accurate translation of the original text: "For the love of money is a root of all kinds of evil."[1]

Another often-repeated biblical quote, used to warn us that having abundant wealth could cause us to be banned from heaven, is: "It is easier for a camel to go through the eye of a needle than for someone who is rich to enter the kingdom of God."[2] And here's another popular one: "What good is it for someone to gain the whole world, yet forfeit their soul?"[3]

Now, I don't want to disrespect the teachings of the Bible or anyone's spiritual beliefs, let me be clear about that. Neither do I purport to be an expert on the Bible or on religious teachings in general. However, because so much of this particular brand of subconscious programming comes from the Christian religious tradition, I do feel that I have to address at least some of these teachings in order to give proper consideration to this particular type of subconscious barrier to wealth.

Notice that the popular rendition of the first quote is, "Money is the root of all evil." According to more accurate, contemporary translations, the Bible talks about the *love* of money—that is, not about money itself, but rather an attitude toward money, a mind-set, if you will. And it talks of this love of money being *a* root of all kinds of evil, but not *the* root.

These are important distinctions, although rather subtle ones—probably a bit too subtle for the subconscious mind to discern. We have to be plainer than that when it comes to programming our subconscious.

We'll come back to the distinction about money mind-set later, when I discuss the character of Ebenezer Scrooge and what I believe to be the true moral of *A Christmas Carol*. But first, let's look at the story in the Bible that generated that quote about the camel.

Know Where I Can Buy a Very Small Camel?

The biblical story about the camel passing through the eye of a needle starts with a young wealthy man who comes to Jesus and asks him what he should do to ensure that he will be saved. Jesus tells him to observe God's commandments. That's pretty simple and clear advice. The young man is not satisfied though. He replies that he has always observed the commandments, kind of implying that surely there must be something more to it than that.

So then Jesus says that there is one thing the young man has not done: "Go, sell everything you have and give to the poor, and you will have treasure in heaven. Then come, follow me."[4]

The young man doesn't appear to be overly pleased with this answer, so off he goes. That's when Jesus makes the comment about the camel and the rich man to his disciples, saying, "It is easier for a camel to go through the eye of a needle than for someone who is rich to enter the kingdom of God."

The disciples are actually pretty shocked by that remark. What? That seems like a pretty steep requirement—does everyone need to give up all their worldly goods in order to be saved? They promptly ask each other, "Who then can be saved?"[5]

And Jesus replies, "With man this is impossible, but not with God; all things are possible with God."[6]

So it seems that the rich are not the only ones who might have trouble getting into heaven on their own steam. Everyone, according to Jesus, needs God's help on that score.

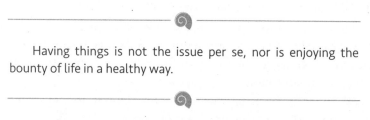

Having things is not the issue per se, nor is enjoying the bounty of life in a healthy way.

It's a very common teaching amongst many of the world's religions, particularly Eastern spiritual traditions, that it is the mental attachment or addiction to material goods (or physical appearance or the satisfaction of physical desires) that poses the real problem. Having things is not the issue per se, nor is enjoying the bounty of life in a healthy way. A psychological (and perhaps spiritual) problem arises when one becomes obsessive, begins to hoard things, or becomes jealous and covetous of what other people have.

Was Jesus maybe trying to teach the young man and his disciples that the most important factor is mind-set or attitude? In the case of the young man, perhaps it was not so much his wealth as his attitude toward that wealth—maybe his attachment to it or his use of it—that was the problem.

The NIV Study Bible, in the notes accompanying that section of Mark, states:

> The man's primary spiritual problem was his wealth, and therefore Jesus' prescription was to rid him of it. There is no indication that Jesus' command to him was meant for all Christians. It applies only to those who have the same spiritual problem.[7]

One of my company's clients named Rudolf was kind enough to read an early draft of this book. He came back to me with some very insightful comments on the topic of the rich man and the camel. Rudolf has agreed for me to include his comments for your benefit:

I start with citing a sentence of the text in Latin:

Mt 19, 22 *cum audisset autem adulescens verbum abiit tristis erat enim habens multas possessiones*

The rich young man is described as *"habens multas possessiones,"* meaning "having many possessions."

You could interpret this in a quantitative manner and contrast it with "having few possessions"; so having a multitude or a lack of possessions belong both to the same absolute category. But you can also interpret it in a qualitative way. This puts the emphasis on the word *having.*

In this line of thought, the contrast to "having" is "being." Being directly relates to the name of Jesus himself, whom the young man is advised to follow. The name Jesus means "I am who I am." So, my interpretation suggests it matters more *who you are* than *what you have.*

So perhaps in this interpretation, when Jesus told the young man to follow him . . . where Jesus's name means "I am who I am" . . . maybe he was telling the young man to follow the path of "being" rather than the path of "having."

Rudolf expanded upon this point:

In other words, my self-worth is innate; it is not derived from external sources or possessions. If you are not worthy (that is, not feeling worthy within) you have no real worth in life.

Seeing it that way, if you wanted to derive your "worthiness" from renouncing any possessions, it would not make a difference, because it does not liberate you from the absolute category "having" and doesn't change your reliance on external influences.

Finding your true self and being yourself will open up the heavens (the plural is used in the Latin!) to you.

A cup serves its purpose by being empty, a human being by being open.

If it's one's attitude or mind-set toward money that matters, then what constitutes a good attitude? That, of course, is a deep philosophical question!

I believe our client Rudolf is onto something when he talks about the empty cup and the importance of being open. Many Eastern spiritual traditions speak of the "beginner's mind" as being vital to spiritual advancement—that is, a mind that is always open to new knowledge and to new ways of looking at things.

Jesus also may have made reference to this kind of mental state when he said, "Truly I tell you, anyone who will not receive the kingdom of God like a little child will never enter it."[8]

Jesus appears to be teaching that a certain kind of innocence in the way that one approaches things is vital. And that would argue for a mind that is free of preconceived notions—even about money.

Mind-Set Matters

It's interesting to note that neuroscientists are now discovering that the brain displays neuroplasticity, meaning that it can continually adapt to and absorb new knowledge, as well as reorganize itself. In fact, people who do not continue to learn new things may actually end up inflicting a kind of damage on their brains.

The brain, it seems, is designed to want to constantly acquire new skills so that it can continue to form new neuronal connections. This allows the brain to combat the fact that the absolute number of neurons it contains declines as we age. Forming new connections between the neurons we've still got is how the aging brain keeps itself fresh and functioning optimally.

People who don't feed their brains by learning new things have been shown to suffer various types of mental atrophy (some of which may become irreversible), resulting in much higher rates of dementia and other cognitive functioning deficits in their senior years.[9] So just speaking from a brain science perspective, having a "beginner's mind" is definitely important. From the Eastern spiritual perspective, it is also a highly valued mental state.

Someone with a beginner's mind does not assume that they already have a full grasp of what is "right" or "wrong." Because of this, they are not dogmatic or closed-minded. They also tend to be more compassionate and forgiving, as they accept that knowing what is right in any given situation is often a complex question. They tend to be kinder to themselves, as well as kinder to others, as they acknowledge that they (like everyone else) are not perfect.

Such people try to navigate life by doing their best and seeing it as a journey of evolution. They continually seek to learn and improve themselves, to find the path that is right for them while trying to tread lightly on the earth . . . rejoicing in the fact that they still don't know everything there is to know and that there is always much left to learn.

Someone who is truly an embodiment of the beginner's mind is able to view life as a fantastic adventure, as a journey that is filled with constant wonder and discovery. They are able to approach life with gusto and savor a variety of experiences—both "good" and "bad"—with the attitude they all teach something valuable.

Sometimes this mental attitude is referred to as "childlike innocence." Many great spiritual masters are said to embody this state, which is distinctly different to being childish. The childlike state is possibly a return to innocence—a state that the wise one returns to having acquired knowledge, having transmuted that knowledge into wisdom, and having used that wisdom to be free from the anxieties and worries that plague most humans. Free of these anxieties, they are able to experience the world with a sense of wonder, joy, and spontaneity akin to that of a child.

In the childish state, before one has much life experience, there exists a rather fragile type of innocence that is only present because one has yet to face many trials or traumas in life. The childlike state, on the other hand, is where one has acquired enough spiritual wisdom to purify, forgive, and let go of the traumas that have been experienced, and thus reclaim the soul's original innocence.

Could Money Actually Make Us Better?

As we have discussed, many people carry the subconscious belief that having money is somehow going to make them a bad person, that it is somehow going to change them and corrupt their character. But is it possible, instead, that having money could actually make you a better person?

Well, that's a hard question to answer on the level of the individual. But it seems that when we look at the data on an aggregate societal level across a range of countries, there is very strong evidence to suggest that having more money could in fact make us better as a group.

How do we measure the concept of becoming "better" people? One social indicator could be measuring the level of violent crimes such as rapes and homicides, and observing if the incidence of these crimes changes as incomes increase (the fewer violent crimes, the better). Another measure could be fewer property crimes such as theft, along with an increase in people's subjective measures of safety and security.

Other indications of improvement could relate to our environment, such as less deforestation, less pollution, and fewer environmental disasters. Some measures may relate to basic physical and emotional health, such as lower infant mortality and suicide rates.

Then there are the yardsticks of educational advancement, like higher literacy or even a greater number of Nobel Prize achievements per capita. And let's not forget subjective well-being measures like people's own ratings of happiness, contentment, and enjoyment of life.

Figure 3 (below) plots the relation between the composite Advanced QOL (Quality of Life) Index of Diener, which aggregates a broad range of social indicators, such as the ones discussed above, and the per capita purchasing power of nations, which is a measure of income. [10]

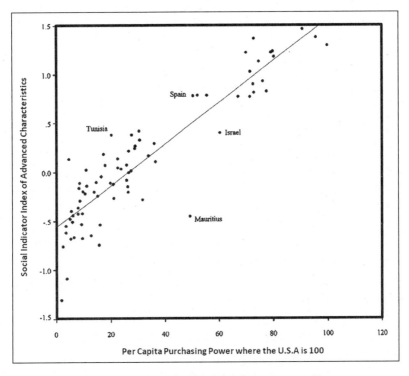

Figure 3: From Diener and Suh (1997): Economic quality of life compared to a Social Indicator Index

There is a strong positive correlation. It's clear from this chart that as the purchasing power per person (income) increases, so does the quality of life across a composite of a wide range of social indicators that can all be argued to represent societal improvement.[11]

In other words, all over the world, across many different cultures and societies, the results are pretty robust: As we get richer, we tend to become better human beings. We steal less, we rape less, and we murder less. We care more about the environment. We care more about health, both our own and that of others. We care more about literacy and education. We also make more scientific advancements, meaning we collectively come up with more solutions to more of the problems facing the world. We win more Nobel Prizes. We feel happier.

In other words, all over the world, across many different cultures and societies, the results are pretty robust: As we get richer, we tend to become better human beings.

We've talked before about the distinction between correlation and causation. Correlation does not equal causation. Just because social prosperity and social well-being tend to go hand in hand, it does not mean that social prosperity is the thing that causes social well-being. It could be the other way around: Societies that have less rape, murder, and other violence may tend to be more prosperous as a result. Either way, it seems that wealth might be good in an aggregate sense. Or at least we can say that prosperity and other good things tend to go hand in hand on the societal level.

I would argue that abundance is good for societies because in the Abundance Mind-Set framework, generosity is a key aspect. When we feel abundant and secure in our sense that there is enough to go around, it's easier to be generous. In this framework it's much more likely that everyone will get their basic needs met.

When we are collectively stuck in the Scarcity Mind-Set, we are afraid of the future, and we are much more likely to hoard what we have, to be protective of it, and to be suspicious and careful of giving too much to others. It's easy to see how this could lead to great disparities in wealth, leaving many participants out in the cold even when the system as a whole is growing and prosperous.

Great disparities in wealth, a potential Scarcity Mind-Set symptom on a societal level, might not be so good for communities. And there is some evidence to back up this idea.

Mind the Gap

In the U.S. there is a lot of wealth disparity, as we will soon see. And this can lead to social problems. Steven Levitt, co-author of the best-selling book *Freakonomics* and currently the William B.

Ogden Distinguished Service Professor of Economics at the University of Chicago, delivered a research paper in 1999 that tracked crime rates and income disparities in Chicago neighborhoods back to the 1970s. This is one of the longest data sets for a study of this kind.[12]

In the early 1970s, the gap between rich and poor was much narrower in Chicago than it had become by the 1990s. So the wealth gap had widened over the time period of the study. Data relating to property crimes showed that these had also become much more prevalent in the poorer neighborhoods over the same period.

The increase in crime in the poorer neighborhoods might be related to dissatisfaction and discontent about societal inequities. However, it's hard to tell whether this is the real cause because higher crime may be linked to other factors like lower education levels, which are also correlated to income. In addition, those on higher incomes can afford to take more precautionary measures against crime, such as installing home and vehicle security systems and moving to safer neighborhoods, including gated communities.

Hence, it's hard to say which statement might be true:

- A disparity in wealth creates *more* crime in poor neighborhoods due to feelings of dissatisfaction.

- The wealth of the rich results in *less* crime being perpetrated against them due to their ability to afford to take precautions and due to behavioral changes like increased education levels reducing crime rates within their own class.

The upshot of all this is that it seems that greater wealth is a good thing when we look at how it affects human behavior on an aggregate societal level as the general income of a nation rises. However, when that rise in income is disproportionately distributed amongst the classes—if the gap between rich and poor widens too much—then things are not quite so rosy.

I think it's possible that the data is telling us that an "abundance" model of wealth is beneficial to society, where everyone gets to participate in the rising prosperity to at least some degree, while a "scarcity" model (where the increase in wealth is hoarded by a few and not shared in a way that benefits the broader population) is perhaps not so good.

When severe disparities arise, so can feelings of injustice and discontent on the part of those who are disadvantaged. If we consider ourselves to be a microcosm of society, then we can relate more directly to how this might be the case. If we lived in a community of 100 people where 20 members held 80 percent of the assets, while the other 80 people had to make do with the remaining 20 percent, there might be some hard feelings about the situation.

Interestingly enough, that's a pretty good representation of the actual wealth distribution in the United States, based on data presented in a 2011 study by Michael Norton from Harvard Business School and Dan Ariely from Duke University (author of the best-selling book *Predictably Irrational*). In the U.S., the richest 20 percent of the population, known as the first quintile, owns about 84 percent of all the assets. The second richest 20 percent (the second quintile) owns about 11 percent of the assets. The third quintile owns about 4 percent of the assets, and the fourth and fifth quintiles *combined* own *less than half a percent* of all the assets. In Figure 4 (below), the actual asset holdings of the fourth and fifth quintiles are so tiny that they are not even visible on the chart![13]

So why is there not more of an uproar from the people about such inequalities? Is it because Americans actually feel that greed is good? Well, according to survey data, apparently not.

Norton and Ariely demonstrate a couple of interesting facts relating to wealth distribution in the U.S. The pair used a random, representative sample of 5,522 online survey respondents drawn from a pool of more than one million Americans. First, they showed that most people in the U.S. vastly underestimate how dramatic the disparity of wealth actually is in their own country. This means that most Americans think they are living in a country that has a far more equitable distribution of wealth than it really does. Second, they showed that most Americans think the ideal distribution of wealth should be even more equitable than their overestimate of what it currently is.

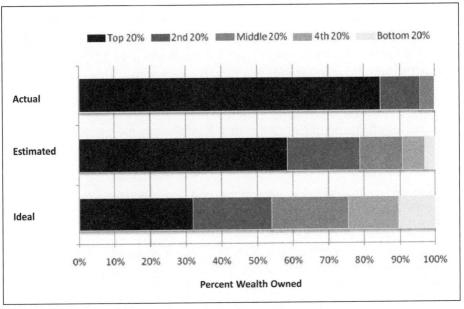

Figure 4: From Norton and Ariely (2011): The actual United States wealth distribution plotted against the estimated and ideal distributions across all respondents

Their results were surprisingly robust and consistent across different types of respondents. Republicans versus Democrats, men versus women, wealthy versus poor—such differences didn't matter as much as we might expect. Regardless of their political orientation, gender, or wealth status, the respondents quite consistently thought that the wealth distribution in the U.S. was already more equitable than it actually is, *and* they felt that it ideally should be even more equitable still.[14]

Note that the reported ideal distribution is still not completely equal. The top quintiles do hold significantly more wealth than the lower quintiles even in the ideal scenario, so Americans do believe in some degree of wealth inequality.

Thinking of incentivized pay scales in the corporate world, for example, it's hard to imagine how total wealth equality in an economy would encourage entrepreneurial behavior and innovation. If there were no financial incentive to innovate, would we do it as much?

At any rate, it seems that Americans on both sides of the ideological spectrum report a preference for a distribution of wealth that retains financial incentives for endeavor and excellence—with some extra reward for reaching the upper quintiles—but that does not see the lower quintiles left with practically none of the wealth. According to Norton and Ariely's research, even though the American people are reporting a preference for a more generous distribution across the classes, that's not the current reality in the U.S.

Democracy Versus Aristocracy

It's worth noting that although many countries today are democracies, most Western cultures developed from aristocracies. In such systems, those of noble birth (the landed gentry) held almost all of the productive assets in the society. In centuries past, these assets were mostly land based.

The landed gentry (lords) were relatively few, and the majority of the population was composed of workers (serfs). The serfs worked the lord's land, while paying the lord rent to live on his land (hence the term *landlord*). The serfs often had little real opportunity for material advancement.

As much as we may feel we have escaped this type of feudal system politically, it seems that not all countries have left it behind in terms of their actual wealth distribution. And this is despite the apparent desire for a more equitable distribution of wealth on the part of their citizenry.

We've talked a lot about how money can provide freedom of choice. The thing is, when we're making personal choices, we don't always consider what's best for the community, the ecology, or the society in which we live—especially when we are operating from a Scarcity Mind-Set, where we are fearful. It can be easy in that frame of mind to do things that just serve our own personal needs but that do not necessarily serve the greater good.

When we see such radical disparities in wealth as the data reveal in the U.S., we might be excused for wondering whether money is the root of all evil. But Norton and Ariely's survey results indicate that this kind of inequity is not what most people consider to be fair. It's not the state of affairs that most people want.

So why is it happening? Could this inequity be traced back to a prevalence of the Scarcity Mind-Set? And if so, what would happen if enough people were to parashift to a more generous Abundance Mind-Set? Would we see a more equitable shift in the wealth distribution as a result? It's a question worth contemplating.

Case Study: Ebenezer Scrooge

The fictional character of Ebenezer Scrooge from Charles Dickens's famous story *A Christmas Carol* is so well-known that he can be considered an archetype of the grumpy old miser. For many people, the character of Scrooge also best represents the belief that money is the root of all evil.

As we look more deeply into the characterization of Ebenezer Scrooge, I will argue that his main problem is not that he has money. It's that he has a Scarcity Mind-Set. He's not coming from an Abundance Mind-Set.

When the story begins, he is basically in a state of emotional lockdown as a result of childhood wounding. He hoards his money, is mean toward his employees, and is perpetually angry and defensive. He doesn't take time to enquire into the lives of others or to connect with them, and so he avoids having to feel either guilt or compassion toward them.

The Ghosts of Christmas Past, Christmas Present, and Christmas Yet to Come appear to Scrooge on Christmas Eve to show him how his mind-set about money is negatively impacting the lives of others, and even his own enjoyment of life.

The Ghost of Christmas Past shows Scrooge how a few defining events were instrumental in molding his character into that of the grumpy old miser. We see that as a child, Scrooge was denied an adequate measure of love and affection, and that this is essentially the emotional wound that sets him on the path to obsessively seeking money as a means to fill the void.

We find out that as a young man, Scrooge let the love of a good woman go simply because she lacked a dowry, thereby sealing his fate to grow old alone and unloved. Throughout his life, his misguided urge to accumulate money as an emotional salve grew like a cancer inside him and ended up clouding his judgment about what was important. He developed a fixation on money that was unhealthy. It was this fixation that corrupted his character, rather than money itself being an inherently corrupting influence.

The Ghost of Christmas Present shows Scrooge that because he is unwilling to pay his employee Bob Cratchit a decent salary, Bob is unable to provide adequate care for his family, and in particular for his ailing son Tiny Tim. Bob is loyal and a good worker, but Scrooge treats him with disrespect and contempt. From the scenes the Ghost of Christmas Present shows him, Scrooge begins to feel remorse for his actions toward Bob.

Scrooge is also shown by the Ghost of Christmas Present how much fun he misses out on due to having refused the invitation of his good-natured nephew, Fred, to share Christmas dinner with his family. Fred, it seems, has been persistently encouraging Scrooge to connect with his family; and despite Scrooge's ill-tempered refusals, Fred appears to take it all in good humor.

The Ghost of Christmas Yet to Come shows Scrooge that upon his death he will not be missed. His grave will be unvisited, and some will even be glad to hear of his passing. He is also shown that Tiny Tim will not survive, largely because of Scrooge's miserly refusal to pay Bob Cratchit a fair wage. Scrooge is horrified, and the lesson of the ghosts is understood. Scrooge pleads with the Ghost of Christmas Yet to Come to please tell him whether or not there is still time for the outcome to be changed, if he can mend his ways.

After spending the night with these three Ghosts, Scrooge wakes the next morning completely transformed. From that moment on he treats others with generosity, respect, and kindness. Scrooge becomes a generous benefactor and friend to Bob Cratchit's family, and Tiny Tim survives as a result. Scrooge attends his nephew's Christmas party, warmly engages with his family, and has fun. Perhaps most important, Scrooge himself becomes infinitely happier as a result of his transformation.

In the three main characters—Scrooge, Bob Cratchit, and Scrooge's nephew, Fred—we see three different combinations of wealth and mind-set.

Scrooge has a great deal of wealth, but when the story opens he lacks an Abundance Mind-Set. He is coming from a position of scarcity. This psychological position is what leads him to be miserly and ill-tempered. His fearful, miserable, and suspicious mind-set is not a result of the money he has accumulated, but because of his early childhood emotional wounding. This combination of having money and a Scarcity Mind-Set is portrayed by Dickens as leading to misery. Note that the words *miserable* and *misery* have the same root as *miser*—a word often used to describe the Scarcity Mind-Set.

Bob Cratchit, on the other hand, is portrayed as having a generous heart, but he lacks the financial means to be generous in practice. As a result, Bob is unable to adequately provide for his family—a fact that gives him much pain. This combination of generosity of spirit and material poverty is also shown by Dickens to be an unhappy one.

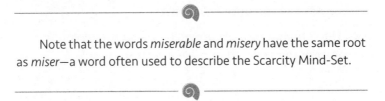

Note that the words *miserable* and *misery* have the same root as *miser*—a word often used to describe the Scarcity Mind-Set.

It is only in the character of Scrooge's nephew, Fred, that we see a man of reasonable financial means who also possesses a generous heart and an abundant nature. Fred demonstrates a love of others, and he also has the financial means to be generous. He displays no inherent love of money. Rather, his relative financial abundance affords him the freedom to express his good-natured, carefree, and fun-loving character.

In the jolly portrayal of Fred's character—and indeed in the portrayal of the happy fruits of Scrooge's own transformation from a Scarcity Mind-Set to an Abundance Mind-Set—Dickens is clearly putting forward that the combination of both material and emotional abundance is the ideal combination.

Hence the moral of Charles Dickens's *A Christmas Carol* is not that money is evil, nor that money corrupts. It was not Ebenezer Scrooge's wealth that corrupted him; it was the emotional wounding that he received in childhood that turned him from happiness and good character. Instead, the moral of the story is that money can be used to do a great deal of good and to facilitate a life of happiness and satisfaction for oneself and for others, as long as one's mind-set is based in Abundance and not in Scarcity.

Digging Deep

1. Have you ever experienced any type of religious fear or guilt when it comes to wealth creation?

2. Do you believe that wealth or money can have a corrupting influence? If so, what do you feel are the key drivers of that corruption? Is it money itself that causes the corruption of spirit?

3. Do you believe that money could facilitate your improving yourself as a person? If so, how?

Action Steps

1. Read (or reread) Charles Dickens's *A Christmas Carol* for yourself to get a sense of each character in more detail. Do the characters remind you of anyone you may have encountered in your own life? Can you think of people who embody for you the three combinations of wealth and mind-set I discussed— material wealth combined with a Scarcity Mind-Set (like Scrooge), poverty combined with generosity of spirit (like Bob Cratchit), and material prosperity combined with an Abundant Mind-Set (like Scrooge's nephew, Fred)?

2. Make a list of some wealthy people (either famous people or ones you personally know) whom you feel have been corrupted. Was money a key factor in their corruption, in your opinion? Or could it be something else? Research their biographies, or if you know them, ask about their history for clues.

3. Make a list of wealthy people whom you feel have not been corrupted. What do you feel was the reason they were able to avoid corruption? Again, research their histories and past influences on their character.

4. Is there a theme in your lists from steps 2 and 3? Now, spend some time in self-reflection: List what steps you could take to ensure that wealth or money would not be a corrupting influence on you. This simple process alone can help to weaken your fears about it, and thereby weaken the grip of this money myth on your mind.

5. Visit www.theabundancecodebook.com to access some extra content about the 7 Money Myths that I have created for you.

CHAPTER TEN

Myth Busting
"As You Think, So Shall You Be"

Have you heard the story about the five monkeys?

Does that sound like the setup for a bad joke? It's not. It's actually an interesting story that goes like this: Scientists conducted an experiment involving five monkeys, a bunch of bananas, and a ladder. They put the five monkeys in a cage with a bunch of bananas hanging from the roof of the cage and a ladder that would allow the monkeys to reach the bananas if they climbed up it. But every time one of the monkeys tried to climb the ladder, the scientists sprayed all of the animals with ice-cold water. The monkeys soon learned that if any one of them went for the bananas, they'd all get an icy bath. Soon, they all stopped trying to get the bananas.

Next, the scientists removed one member from the original group of monkeys and replaced it with a different monkey that had never been sprayed with cold water. Of course the first thing this new monkey did was try to climb the ladder and get the bananas. But the other monkeys, expecting this activity to trigger an unpleasant soaking for them all, instantly pulled the new monkey off the ladder and beat him up. Every time the new monkey tried to climb the ladder, the other monkeys pulled him down and beat him. So he soon also learned not to go for the bananas.

Then the scientists removed another member of the original group of five monkeys and replaced it with a second new monkey that had also never been sprayed with cold water. The same scenario ensued, with the other monkeys beating him when he tried to climb the ladder and get the bananas. Only this time, the first new monkey, who had never once been sprayed by ice water, also participated in the beatings—even though he couldn't know *why* it wasn't a good idea to go for the bananas.

The scientists continued replacing the monkeys one by one in this manner until none of the original group remained. All of the animals in the cage now were new monkeys that had never been sprayed with cold water, and yet they continued to beat any monkey that attempted to climb the ladder and fetch the bananas.

And thus ended all attempts by the monkeys to get the bananas. If the circumstances changed over time—for example, if the scientists decided they wouldn't spray the monkeys anymore, or even if the scientists had all packed up and gone home—it wouldn't matter. The behavior was set, predetermined by the beliefs of a group of monkeys who weren't even in the room anymore!

Wow. It makes you think, doesn't it?

But . . . is this a true story? Well, no. I'm pretty sure it's not. I can't find any academic reference to an experiment like this. There have been many scientific experiments about behavioral conditioning conducted on animals, and many of them have used monkeys, but this is not one of them.

Even though it seems that no such experiment was ever conducted, the story has become a myth that has been told and retold and propagated on the Internet. It has kind of taken on a life of its own. I have heard it from various people, and each time it's been related to me as if it is a factual scientific study that actually took place. I even found a great cartoon depiction of it on Vimeo.[1] And each time I've heard this story recounted, I've seen the people listening to the story nodding their heads as if to say, "Yeah, that makes total sense."

This is the moment when I confess that I also believed this story at first. Once, I even showed the cartoon to a room of 400 people as a part of a presentation I was giving. It sounded completely plausible to me until I took the time to look it up and check on the facts of the matter.

Now what I find most fascinating about this story is that it speaks to a universal behavioral phenomenon, which is the human tendency to not only create but also to believe in *myths*.

The Power of Myth

Anthropologists have documented that there are some features of culture, language, behavior, and society that exist universally. What that means is that they can be found across all known cultures and societies, both primitive and evolved. These features are called the "human universals."

One of the human universals is the creation of myths and stories. It seems that we human beings are wired to create stories that resonate with some sense of societal, behavioral, or cultural "truth." Myths help us to understand how things work in our society, in our culture, in our tribe. Amongst other things, myths illustrate morals and a sense of right and wrong, and they help to guide our behavior. Creating myths is not only natural; research shows that it's a universally human thing to do.

One conclusion we can draw from the universality of myths is that they can be very powerful. They reach deep into the human psyche, and they operate on a subconscious level, influencing our conscious behavior in a myriad of ways. It doesn't matter which culture or social group we are from, we all create myths. And although myths are usually not factually (or "externally") true, a myth will often become popular when it tells a compelling and entertaining story about something that we hold to be *internally* true.

The reason why this story about the monkeys became a successful myth is probably because it reflects back to us something that we perceive to have truth. We all know people who tend *not* to question the way things are done, even if that way doesn't make a lot of sense. So perhaps the monkey story has spread so widely because it speaks to something that resonates with what we have seen in the behavior of people we all know (and, in some cases, work with): the truth that we can easily become conditioned to accept ideas that are very limiting.

And this sounds kind of like the way in which many of us have been conditioned to believe and internalize the 7 Money Myths.

Before We Go Busting . . .

As I mentioned in the Introduction, the purpose of examining each of the 7 Money Myths one by one, as we have done in the last seven chapters, is twofold:

1. To help you identify whether or not you might be holding these or similar subconscious beliefs that may be thwarting your conscious desire to achieve financial freedom

2. To introduce an element of *doubt* regarding the validity of these commonly held limiting beliefs, in order to begin viewing them as *myths* that do not have to be true for you if you don't want them to be

If you want to weaken the hold of limiting beliefs on your subconscious, the introduction of doubt about those beliefs is a very important first step. So we've had a good look at these myths about money, and we've used the power of our logical minds to question their validity. We've introduced doubt.

But the introduction of doubt alone is unlikely to do the full job. As you've learned, it's also important to overwrite the old limiting beliefs with new beliefs that are going to be more supportive of your goals. In other words, you need to perform a mental software update.

Here's an important question: *How?* How do you change your subconscious beliefs? I'll come back to this question very soon, I promise. First, we need to take a little detour though . . . because before we go messing around with our subconscious programming, we need to talk about what constitutes a well-formed belief. If we are performing a software update, we don't want to introduce any bugs or glitches. We want to make sure the new programming is of high quality.

The Characteristics of Well-Formed Beliefs

We like to have familiar feelings in our life, because that's how we know that we're ourselves. If we change what is familiar, if we change what we believe and how we habitually respond to situations, then we're essentially changing who we are.

That means that when you start changing beliefs, it's important to *take care.* You are shifting your mental programming, so you want to make sure you shift it in the right direction. Make sure your new beliefs are well formed so that they don't have any unintended side effects.

For example, let's say we are changing the "easy come, easy go" belief. How about replacing that belief with something like, "Money flows into my life easily and stays"?

Well, that might be a belief that is still limiting. It might have the unintended side effect of not letting you use much of the wealth that has flowed into your life so easily. If it all has to "stay," then that could mean that the money can't be spent. If it can't be spent, then that's going to constrain you when it comes to enjoying your wealth. You might end up hoarding it all.

A better belief might be something like, "Money flows into my life easily, and my wealth continues to grow." That's a belief that does not preclude spending some of the money that flows into your life; and the condition that your wealth continues to grow ensures that it is not going to be an "easy come, easy go" situation where it all flows out again. An easy inflow with some accumulation is then allowed for, without your having to hoard.

According to Tim Hallbom and Kris Hallbom—Neuro-Linguistic Programming (NLP) experts who run an excellent money belief change workshop called The WealthyMind Program—well-formed beliefs have the following characteristics:

- They are stated in the positive.

- They add behavioral choices; they do not take choices away.

- They are beliefs and not behaviors.

- They are stated in simple (almost childlike) language.

- They are ecological—meaning you cannot predict a downside to holding this empowering belief.

- They are process oriented rather than results oriented.

- They empower with possibility.[2]

I would add a couple of other criteria to this mix as well:

- They are stated in the present tense.

- If possible, they are associated with visual imagery.

Using the same example again, let's say you suspect that you carry the limiting belief of "easy come, easy go," and you wish to install the more positive and supportive belief that "money flows into my life easily, and my wealth continues to grow."

First, you need to make sure that the new belief is well formed. Here's a checklist based on the Hallboms' characteristics of well-formed beliefs, plus the two additional criteria that I've added. The comments evaluate our proposed new belief.

Well-Formed Beliefs Checklist		
Criteria		**Comments**
Is it stated in the positive?	✓	The new belief is phrased to avoid using the words *not, without,* and *instead of.*
Is it stated in the present tense?	✓	The new belief is phrased to avoid putting the realization off into the future, avoiding words such as *will, going to,* and *in the future.* It is phrased as if it is already happening.
Is it stated in simple (almost childlike) language?	✓	The simpler the better, because the subconscious responds best to simplistic language.

Is it describing a belief and not a behavior?	✓	An example of a belief is "Money flows into my life easily, and my wealth continues to grow"; an example of a behavior would be "When money comes to me, I invest it."
Does it add choices and not take choices away?	✓	Yes. I can now choose how to spend and/or invest my money, knowing that more will come and my wealth will grow . . . rather than it having to all flow out of my life right away.
Is there no predictable downside to holding this new belief?	✓	It's difficult to think of one. However, this question always deserves careful contemplation.
Is it process oriented rather than results oriented?	✓	The process described here is "Money flows into my life easily," whereas a results-based statement might be something like, "I win $100 in a raffle."
Does it empower with possibility?	✓	Yes, although it does try to take away the negative possibility of losing money as easily as gaining it.
If possible, is it associated with visual imagery?	✓	I could associate a simple image such as money being attracted to me like a magnet.

I can't emphasize enough the importance of making sure that your new beliefs are well formed. If you are going to do subconscious reprogramming work, it's vital to ensure that the code you are inputting is of high quality. If you want more freedom, then make sure you do not limit yourself in any way.

Your own *Abundance Code* is a set of subconscious beliefs that will give you choices and allow you to have freedom in your life—financially, emotionally, and spiritually. You need to choose for yourself what your own *Abundance Code* beliefs will be. No one else can do that for you. I'm just guiding you through the process.

Once you have identified your own *Abundance Code,* it's also a good idea to look at what habits may support you in cementing and stabilizing your new beliefs.

The Habit Loop

To understand habits, we must draw on our knowledge of beliefs. The reason beliefs are stored subconsciously is because they are part of our survival mechanisms. We never actually install a subconscious belief unless we perceive that it serves or protects us in some way.

I'll come back to this idea of the *service* of our beliefs, because it's really important. In the meantime, let's just say that tampering with beliefs that serve or protect us is perceived by the psyche as dangerous. If we can't access them, we can't mess with them. So for the safety and integrity of the system, these beliefs are stored in the vault of our subconscious mind and housed in the limbic part of the brain.

Beliefs drive habitual responses, which dictate an enormous amount of our behavior. Our conscious mind only processes about 5 percent of the information we receive. The other 95 percent is processed by the subconscious according to rule-based protocols or programs, protocols that include our beliefs, which drive our habits.

Most people have a very hard time changing their ingrained habits. Ask anyone who has recovered from an addiction, and they will tell you that it's not easy.

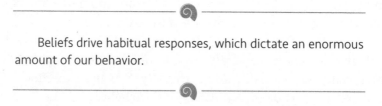

Beliefs drive habitual responses, which dictate an enormous amount of our behavior.

The latest research has shown that trying to remove old habits is very difficult, but that they can be altered surprisingly simply if we can identify the cue that triggers the habitual behavior and the reward that follows it.

In *The Power of Habit,* Charles Duhigg discusses something that he calls "the habit loop." According to Duhigg, every ingrained habit follows a series of three steps:

1. A cue that signals the behavior is about to commence

2. A routine behavior

3. A reward for doing the behavior[3]

For example, someone addicted to smoking might smoke cigarettes when they drink with their friends (that's a cue followed by a routine behavior), and the reward they get is the physiological stimulus that comes from the nicotine as well as a sense of bonding and camaraderie with their friends.

Someone who has a regular habit of exercising might have a cue like lacing up their running shoes or changing into their exercise clothes, followed by their exercise routine, after which they receive a physiological reward of endorphin release in their body. They may also reward themselves with some kind of treat afterward or by measuring their progress and feeling a sense of achievement.

The habit loop is powered by a craving for the reward. The repeated experience that if and when the cue happens, we do the routine behavior, then we will get the desired reward is the loop that programs the habit into our subconscious operating system. Thus, whenever the cue happens, the behavior kicks in automatically and we don't even think about it.

Because habitual behaviors are, by their very nature, responses that we don't think about, it's extremely difficult to stop them once a cue has been triggered. However, what you can do is substitute a different second step—change the associated routine behavior—which essentially covers over the old routine with a new one. In other words, it seems that when it comes to our mental programming, it's hard to delete habitual programs, but we can overwrite and update them relatively easily.

The reward for the habitual behavior is whatever *service* the behavior provides to us. The service or reward is an important aspect, because that is the thing we come to crave; and every time we get it by doing the habitual behavior, this reinforces the strength of the habit loop.

Let's come back to the smoking example. Any addicted smoker who has had a habit of smoking when they drink with their friends will tell you that this cue can be a powerful obstacle when trying to give up cigarettes. Even after the physiological addiction to nicotine is broken (which only takes a few days), the routine of smoking when drinking with friends (the cue) is still a powerful habit loop.

There are two ways to deal with this. One is to avoid the cue altogether—and in this case that means avoiding social drinking situations. That's a hard choice, because many people like to drink socially, and a big reward of that is bonding with their friends. Avoiding the cue is a strategy that does work though; and that means in order to succeed at giving up smoking, some people take the added step of giving up both drinking and socializing.

The problem with this approach is that there is a great cost involved. The new reward of improved health through quitting smoking can feel small in comparison to the loss of the fun and bonding that comes from socializing with friends. That imbalance of cost versus benefit can set up the whole strategy of "cue avoidance" for failure.

A different approach might be to follow the cue with a different routine behavior that gives a similar reward. For example, if the unwanted habit loop is something like this:

1. Cue = drinking and socializing with friends

2. Routine behavior = smoking

3. Reward = physiological stimulus, bonding with friends

The new habit loop could be modified to:

1. Cue = drinking and socializing with friends

2. Routine behavior = eating peanuts

3. Reward = physiological stimulus, bonding with friends

We retain the same cue, and we keep the same or a very similar reward, but we change the routine behavior in the middle. According to Charles Duhigg, this is known as the golden rule of habit change. Here's how it works:

- Use the same cue

- Provide the same reward

- Change the routine[4]

Now let's look at how changing our beliefs might relate to Duhigg's habit loop and the golden rule, since our beliefs *drive* many of our habitual behaviors.

One of the findings of Duhigg's research on habit loops is that although under most circumstances it's relatively easy to substitute a new routine into an existing habit loop, when people are put under conditions of stress, the old habit loop (with the old unwanted routine behavior) can suddenly reemerge. At times like these, it turns out that the factor that determines whether or not the old unwanted habit is able to successfully reassert itself or not comes down to belief.[5]

If I *change the belief* that drives the habit loop, and then also *change the routine behavior* associated with that habit, then I can *achieve lasting change.*

Quite simply, if the new and more desirable habit loop is not also backed up by a new supportive belief, then the new habit loop is very likely to break down in times of stress.

Let's take the belief "I have to work hard for my money." This belief may drive a habit loop that looks something like this:

1. Cue = get up on a weekday

2. Routine behavior = work hard all day

3. Reward = get money and a sense of achievement

There is nothing in this subconscious habit loop that contradicts the underlying belief that drives it. If I get up, work hard, and get money, then the belief is verified.

The subconscious mind does not have the ability to point out to me that maybe I don't *have* to work hard to get money—that maybe there are other ways to get money that don't involve working hard. No. That is not the role of the subconscious. It simply executes orders. That is all it is designed to do, and it does not provide feedback or reprogramming suggestions.

If I want to install a new habit loop and ensure that it will stick, I need to also identify and change the underlying belief to one that will be supportive of my new desired habit. I have to identify the errors in programming and correct them—either by myself or with the aid of a trained belief-change therapist.

If I *change the belief* that drives the habit loop, and then also *change the routine behavior* associated with that habit, then I can *achieve lasting change.*

Let's say I am able to change the belief to "I make money easily doing what I love" (and don't worry, we'll talk about how to accomplish such a belief change later on in this chapter). At the same time, I want to take care of the way that my habits interplay with my beliefs. So the new belief may then drive a new behavioral habit loop that looks like this:

1. Cue = get up on a weekday

2. Routine behavior = do what I love doing all day

3. Reward = get money and a sense of achievement

Knowing how the habit loop works gives us a behavioral perspective on changing beliefs. When we are doing belief-change work on ourselves, it's a good idea to also have a look at the habit loop associated with the old belief and insert a modified habit loop for the desired new belief. If the new belief drives a habit loop that keeps the old cue and the old reward, but simply changes the routine behavior in the middle, then that's a change that is likely to work. If not, then we can choose the other way to get the behavioral change, which is often more difficult to achieve in practice: completely avoiding the cue for the old habit loop.

Beliefs and Associated Habit Loops

Now let's take a look once more at some of the limiting beliefs about money and wealth that we have examined in this book and some possible new beliefs that could be used to overwrite those limiting programs. Let's also examine some possible habit loop examples and how they might change as we install the new belief. The examples I provide are not necessarily the *only* habit loops that could be in place, and indeed yours may be quite different to these. They are just illustrative examples.

If you are doing belief-change work on yourself, try to identify the habit loops that you have associated with your beliefs so that you can not only change the belief, but also replace the routine behavior in your habit loop with a behavior that is more positive and supportive of your goals.

The following table compares some limiting beliefs and examples of habit loops that could be associated with those beliefs and provides some examples of empowering belief affirmations and possible new habit loops.

Creating New Habit Loops in Support of New Beliefs

Old Limiting Belief	Old Habit Loop Example	New Empowering Belief Affirmation	New Habit Loop Example
"Money doesn't grow on trees."	1. Cue = money comes in 2. Routine = don't spend much or share much because of belief in scarcity 3. Reward = feel safe	"The world is an abundant place, and I share in that abundance." "As I spend money, even more money comes back to me."	1. Cue = money comes in 2. Routine = spend or share generously because of belief in abundance 3. Reward = feel safe and have a new experience
"Time is money."	1. Cue = get up 2. Routine = exchange time for money 3. Reward = get money	"My money makes more money for me, and managing this requires little of my time."	1. Cue = get up 2. Routine = spend very small amount of time overseeing investments 3. Reward = get money
"I have to do something worthy to deserve what I get."	1. Cue = get something or work toward getting something 2. Routine = do something "worthy" 3. Reward = feel deserving	"I deserve to be financially free." "I deserve to have the things that money can buy."	1. Cue = get something or work toward getting something 2. Routine = do whatever I want 3. Reward = feel innately deserving

"It takes money to make money."	1. Cue = don't have enough money for A, B, or C 2. Routine = stress avoidance activity (drinking, watching TV, smoking, texting, checking social media constantly, etc.) 3. Reward = feel a very temporary relief from stress	"I create abundance for myself easily and free of stress."	1. Cue = don't have enough money for A, B, or C 2. Routine = abundance-creation activity (take action toward abundance goal) 3. Reward = feel relief from stress
"The rich get richer, while the poor get poorer."	1. Cue = not getting ahead financially 2. Routine = maintain current knowledge, continue existing actions 3. Reward = feel validated (no improvement in financial circumstances)	"I am financially free."	1. Cue = not getting ahead financially 2. Routine = seek out new knowledge, take new action 3. Reward = feel validated (improvement in financial circumstances)
"Easy come, easy go."	1. Cue = get money easily 2. Routine = lose all of the money quickly 3. Reward = feel validated (evidence collected of belief being externally "verified")	"Money comes easily to me, and my wealth continues to grow."	1. Cue = get money easily 2. Routine = invest some or all of the money and watch it grow 3. Reward = feel validated (evidence collected of belief being externally "verified")

"Money won't make me happy."	1. Cue = desire something that costs money, feel discomfort about not having it 2. Routine = suppress desire by telling myself I don't really want it, and do nothing to attain it 3. Reward = feel slightly better from suppressing the desire, but also somewhat hopeless	"Money allows me to access a range of fun and fulfilling experiences." "I make money easily doing what I love." "I get a sense of significance and contribution from doing the things I love to do."	1. Cue = desire something that costs money, feel discomfort about not having it 2. Routine = allow the desire to grow and develop an action plan to attain it 3. Reward = feel better through a sense of accomplishment and hope
"Money can't buy me love."	1. Cue = desire a shared experience with friends or loved ones that costs money or that I may need to fund 2. Routine = suppress the desire by telling myself it won't be that fun or fulfilling to share that experience anyway, and do nothing to attain it 3. Reward = feel slightly better but also less empowered	"I am surrounded by people who love me for who I am."	1. Cue = desire a shared experience with friends or loved ones that costs money or that I may need to fund 2. Routine = allow the desire to grow and develop an action plan to attain it 3. Reward = feel better and more empowered

"Money is the root of all evil."	1. Cue = desire money and feel guilt about that (because of the underlying belief that such desires are evil) 2. Routine = suppress the desire 3. Reward = feel slightly better, mainly more "righteous"	"I make money with integrity."	1. Cue = desire money and feel no guilt about that (because the underlying belief has been shifted) 2. Routine = allow the desire to grow and develop an action plan to attain it 3. Reward = feel better and empowered

Subconscious Simplicity

Our subconscious minds are not terribly subtle. It is our cerebral cortex—which developed much later in our evolution as a species than our original reptilian limbic brain—that has all the powers of subtlety. The cerebral cortex is where our conscious and rational thought takes place. But it is likely that our limbic brain houses many of our subconscious programs, our ingrained patterns and habits, which have been reduced to simple behavioral loops that run on autopilot.[6]

For our subconscious to be able to code behavior in the limbic brain, complex ideas must be reduced to very basic commands in order to be simple enough for that system. It's basically kind of an "if A, then B" automatic reaction loop that we don't even need to think about. The limbic brain doesn't really accommodate ambiguous options like "Well, sometimes it's like A . . . but on the other hand, sometimes it's like C or D . . . it depends . . . it's complicated."

Let's take the belief that money won't make you happy as an example. In this limbic reduction process, it's very easy for a complex and somewhat subtle idea like "Money *alone* does not necessarily bring about happiness, even though it can help; it probably takes more than just money to experience meaning, joy, and happiness in life . . ." to get reduced and coded in our subconscious as "money ≠ happy" (that ≠ symbol means "does not equal"), and it may even get miscoded as "money = not happy."

A subtle difference in coding at the limbic (subconscious) level can cause a big difference when it comes to practical application and outcomes—a difference that may actually mean we prevent ourselves from having much money!

So if we have ended up with a miscoded subconscious belief about money, what can we do about that?

Reframing

It may be helpful to reframe our goals relating to money. Reframing is a technique used in two processes I mentioned earlier: Neuro-Linguistic Programming (NLP) and also in cognitive behavior therapy (CBT). It's a technique where you take an event or an outcome that has a negative belief association and reposition it so that it's associated with a concept or an idea that does not have a negative belief attached to it.

Essentially, an event has no meaning beyond what we give it based on our beliefs, values, likes, and dislikes. Reframing is about changing the way the event is perceived in order to change what it means to us.

For example, when it comes to the question of whether or not more money will make us happier, many of us have already been programmed to believe that it won't. So what if we reframe the question? What if instead of making it about having more money, we make it about having more freedom or more choices in life? This kind of reframing makes it easier for us to see clearly the relationship between the goal and our happiness.

Moving the focus off money (and off working hard to get that money) can allow us to find new ways to generate freedom and choice in our lives.

A focus on freedom and choice can allow us to pursue and use money in a way that does not force us to compromise by working harder and having less time. Less time generally means less freedom to do the things we love. The constraint of not enough time leaves us with less ability to choose to spend time on activities that we find fulfilling, even if we happen to have enough money to do those things. Moving the focus off money (and off working hard to get that money) can allow us to find new ways to generate freedom and choice in our lives.

While we may be programmed to think that we have to work hard for our money or that time is money, we might not be suffering from the same type of programming when it comes to freedom or choices. Reframing in this way can help us to think outside the box of our preprogrammed beliefs about money.

Let's free ourselves up to think about innovative ways to bring freedom and choice into our lives . . . ways that don't necessarily require us to work too hard or give up too much of our precious time.

7 More Techniques for Changing Subconscious Beliefs

Belief change is a popular topic, and entire books and courses have been devoted to it. So before I go on, I would like to recognize some excellent resource material on beliefs and how to change them:

- *Think and Grow Rich,* by Napoleon Hill, is a classic book first published in 1937. It illustrates the power of beliefs and winning habits based on Hill's personal interviews with and case studies of some of the richest and most successful businessmen in America at the time.

- *The Power of Your Subconscious Mind,* by Joseph Murphy, is another classic. First published in 1963, it's full of practical techniques for reprogramming the subconscious mind and has many case-study examples.

- *Beliefs: Pathways to Health and Well-Being,* by Robert Dilts, Tim Hallbom, and Suzi Smith, provides a Neuro-Linguistic Programming perspective on beliefs.

- *The WealthyMind Program* is a belief-change workshop available on DVD, conducted by NLP experts Tim Hallbom and Kris Hallbom, which focuses specifically on identifying limiting beliefs that relate to money and how to change them.

- *The Power of Habit: Why We Do What We Do and How to Change,* by Charles Duhigg, published in 2012, is a great summary of the latest research on how we form habits, how knowledge of the habit loop provides a road map for change, and also the importance of belief in ensuring that habit change sticks even under conditions of stress.

The following sections describe some belief-change techniques that I have studied. They are all techniques that I've used on myself—either by myself or with the help of a therapist—at one time or another. The list is by no means exhaustive. I'm sure there are lots of other belief-change protocols that work.

I begin by describing some simple and effective belief-change techniques that you can try at home and then move on to techniques that may require facilitation by an experienced and qualified practitioner.

This is the "how to" guide for belief change that I promised you earlier!

1. The Sleepy-Mind Affirmation Method

When we are dropping off to sleep at night, and also when we are still drowsy and just waking up in the morning, the subconscious mind is in a very impressionable state. It's as if the subconscious is closer to the surface at these times and can be more easily accessed for reprogramming. This is a great time to overwrite an old belief and install a new one.[7]

Write the new belief statement (or affirmation) on a piece of paper and keep it beside your bed. Remember to use the checklist provided earlier to ensure that your new belief statement is well formed!

Read the new belief statement aloud to yourself when you first get into bed at night, and then lie back and repeat it to yourself over and over in your mind as you relax and drop off to sleep.

Write the new belief on a piece of paper and keep it beside your bed. Read it aloud to yourself when you get into bed at night, as you drop off to sleep, and again first thing in the morning as you are waking up.

Also imagine what your life will be like with the new belief in place. For example, if your new belief is, "Money flows into my life easily, and my wealth continues to grow," how would it feel for you to have that in your life? Allow yourself to become immersed in that feeling. And how would your daily life look in this new state if you were able to watch a video of yourself? Form some mental pictures of it.

When you wake up, pick up the piece of paper as soon as your eyes open and read it aloud to yourself again. Keep repeating it to yourself mentally for as long as possible while you get up and start your day, allow yourself to feel the associated emotion as if you already have that state of being in your life, and allow some mental pictures of yourself in that state to play in your mind.

You can also continue to repeat this mental process during the day whenever you remember.

2. The Relaxation Affirmation Method

This is similar to the sleepy-mind method, but it can be done at any time throughout the day. Simply get yourself into a relaxed state of mind and then begin repeating the new belief affirmation over and over in your mind.

You can induce a state of relaxation by sitting in a comfortable chair, dimming the lights or closing the blinds, or perhaps lighting a candle or putting on some relaxing music.

Clear your mind by letting your thoughts drift across your mind like clouds in the sky.

Now take yourself to a safe and happy place in your mind. Use a mental image of a place that represents a place of peace, safety, and happiness for you. Perhaps you are in a beautiful sunlit meadow. Perhaps you are on a beach at sunrise with the gentle pounding rhythm of waves rolling in . . . or maybe you are sitting on the bank of a beautiful, bubbling stream with dragonflies darting about and the sound of birds chirping in the trees. It doesn't matter where you choose to make this special place, as long as you feel safe, peaceful, and relaxed when you go there in your mind.

For the purposes of being able to induce this state of relaxation quickly at will, whenever and wherever you want to, it helps to make it a habit of always going to the same place in your mind when you do this exercise. The more often you practice going to this safe place and relaxing there, the quicker and easier it will become for you to enter the state of relaxation.

Once you have reached that special place, take a few slow, deep breaths and relax . . .

Once you have entered a state of relaxation, begin repeating your new belief statement over and over, either out loud or in your mind.

You may want to perform a mental cleansing ritual that represents washing away the cares of the conscious world. For example, if you are mentally sitting beside a stream, you could reach into the crystal clear current, scoop up some water, and splash it on your face. Or if you're by the ocean, maybe see yourself going for a cleansing swim. Imagine all of your worries and stress being washed away, and then come out and bask on the sand in the warm sun. If you're in a meadow, maybe feel the breeze blowing through your hair and taking away all of your cares with it.

Once you have entered a state of relaxation, begin repeating your new belief statement over and over, either out loud or in your mind.

Again, imagine what your life will be like with the new belief in place. For example, if your new belief is, "Money flows into my life easily, and my wealth continues to grow," how would it feel to have that in your life? What would it feel like *not* to have to worry about where your next paycheck is going to come from? Would you feel lighter, like a weight was lifting off your shoulders? Allow that feeling to spread throughout your awareness. Allow it to make you smile. And what would your daily life look like? How would it be different? Allow yourself to play it through in mental pictures like a movie in your mind.

The longer you can do this for the better—but it doesn't have to be a big production if you don't have a lot of time. Even just a few minutes spent this way a couple of times a day can be an incredibly powerful belief-change protocol.

3. Vision Boards

The subconscious mind loves imagery, simple words, and feelings. So when it comes to envisioning your desired state of being—whether it is financial freedom, a fulfilling romantic relationship, or anything else—using pictures, simple phrases, and feelings is often the best way to communicate to the subconscious mind.

There are three types of perceptual processing systems: visual, auditory, and kinesthetic. Basically, we can only process what we see, hear, or feel. And each of us will tend to favor one type of processing system over the others.

I find that imagery is the most effective way to communicate with and program my subconscious. Images provide a type of pre-verbal command to my subconscious. For me, this is like taking the condition that the belief affirmation be stated in simple language and going one step further. Much more information can be conveyed to my subconscious via an image than can be effectively conveyed using a statement. As they say, a picture is worth a thousand words.

I find that imagery is the most effective way to communicate with and program my subconscious.

However, I am a visual person. If you happen to be more auditory, then using well-formed belief affirmations about your desired outcome may work better for you. If you're more kinesthetic, then it may be most important for you to imagine what your desired outcome is going to *feel* like. And because most of us use all of these processing systems to some extent, we can combine their power and do all three.

One very powerful technique is to make an inventory of the new beliefs that you wish to install and look for images that represent those new beliefs in your mind. We talked about this in the Action Steps section of Chapter 2, when we discussed finding and clipping out images and putting them in an "ideal life" file. You can also clip out simple words or phrases that represent aspects of your ideal life. Maybe words like *freedom, fun,* or *love what I do.* Now it's time to take those and arrange the images into a collage. This is called a vision board.

Hang your vision board anywhere you'll be sure to see it multiple times during the day—like in the toilet, for example! Don't be precious about it. Use your daily habits to your advantage when it comes to belief change. While you look at your vision board, try to imagine how having everything in the collage will make you feel.

What kinds of images could you choose? Well, a picture of a magnet with money being attracted to it may represent for you the belief that "money comes into my life easily." A picture of someone like you looking happy, spending time with their partner or friends while cruising on a yacht, or maybe skiing, is an image that may sum up a few different positive beliefs for you:

- I am financially free.
- I am surrounded by people who love me for who I am.
- Money allows me to access a range of fulfilling experiences.

If you want to put words on your board, too, make sure you trim them back to the core idea.

- "I am financially free" might be reduced to *money* and *free* or *abundance*.
- "I am surrounded by people who love me for who I am" might be reduced to *I am loved*.
- "Money allows me to access a range of fulfilling experiences" might be reduced to *Love life*.

Try to cover as many belief affirmations about money and your ideal life as you can with your vision board. You can keep adding to it if you want or create multiple collages that you can put in various places at home, on your desk at work, or even in the car.

4. Mind Movies

It's very powerful if you can play in your mind imagery representing your new belief affirmations and ideal life as a mental movie. Visualize what it will look like when your belief becomes a reality. Visualize yourself achieving your dreams.

For example, if one of your new belief affirmations is "Money flows into my life easily, and my wealth continues to grow," you could turn that into a mental movie by imagining yourself looking at your bank statement (or perhaps checking your account balance online) and seeing the numbers rapidly and constantly increasing.

Visualize what it will look like when your belief becomes a reality. Visualize yourself achieving your dreams.

This is a dynamic image because the numbers are changing all the time, going up and up, so it's a mental movie rather than a static picture. Play this movie to yourself in your mind as often as possible.

Another way to make a type of mind movie is to compile a slide presentation of positive belief imagery. This is a like a vision board where the images are arranged into a sequence, with the belief affirmations attached as well.

A simple way to make a mind movie is to import digital images that represent your new beliefs into a PowerPoint or Keynote slide presentation and write the belief statement on the slide with the image. Then save it and play the presentation to yourself as a slideshow a few times a day.

You can also subscribe to online services relatively cheaply in order to produce a more sophisticated and customized mind movie, complete with music. One such product is available at www.mindmovies.com. (I have no affiliation with this site; I only mention it because I've used it and I like it.) They have some pre-made mind movies available to help you jump-start the process, or you can customize your own. They also sell software that allows you to play your mind movie subliminally all day long on your computer.

Subliminal programming is very powerful. The Mind Movies subliminal software basically takes your mind movie and allows you to turn down the opacity and the volume on the soundtrack to make it kind of see-through and very quiet. This way it can be playing in the background so that it's perceptible to your subconscious mind, but not perceptible on a level that is consciously distracting. If you want to, you can play your mind movie all day long in a continuous loop while you work.

5. Hypnotherapy

Hypnotherapy has long been used as a technique to reprogram the subconscious mind. It is actually a similar process to the sleepy-mind and relaxation techniques (as these are types of self-hypnosis), but is done with a trained hypnotherapist.

Your hypnotherapist will guide you into a deep hypnotic, or trance, state and then make suggestions directly to your subconscious. Once the suggestions have been "installed," the therapist will slowly guide you out of the hypnotic trance state and back to your regular waking conscious state.

Your hypnotherapist will guide you into a deep hypnotic, or trance, state and then make suggestions directly to your subconscious.

Make sure you use a fully qualified hypnotherapist; and before they induce the trance state, thoroughly discuss the type of hypnotic suggestions you would like installed. All the caveats about making sure the beliefs and suggestions are well formed apply here.

If you don't want to go to the effort of finding a hypnotherapist, you could seek out hypnotherapy CDs or audio files. There are many available online that can be used to guide you into a trance state and install wealth-creation hypnotic suggestions.

The problem with this approach is that you may not know in advance what hypnotic suggestions are being made, and you probably won't be able to check them to make sure they are well formed and customized to fit your personal goals.

6. Neuro-Linguistic Programming (NLP)

Neuro-Linguistic Programming is a field of study that was cofounded by John Grinder and Richard Bandler in the 1970s. It seeks to model specifically how behaviors are coded in the mind. It provides a framework that links neurological processes (neuro), language (linguistic), and behavior patterns that have been learned through experience (programming).

NLP has not been particularly well-received by the scientific community, but it is widely practiced as a belief-change protocol and has a lot of anecdotal support as being effective when undertaken by an experienced and well-trained practitioner. I have personally had a lot of success with NLP for belief change. It has helped me to overwrite many of the unhelpful and limiting beliefs that I grew up with.

My NLP therapist is excellent, has a master's in counseling, and was personally trained in NLP by John Grinder. At one point, my therapist wanted to study for a doctorate in counseling with an examination of the efficacy of NLP therapeutic techniques as her proposed thesis topic. The supervisors of the doctoral program she was applying to rejected that topic because they said it was not a scientifically recognized therapeutic technique.

That's kind of like the problem of the chicken and the egg, isn't it? It seems to be saying that NLP is not scientifically recognized because there is a lack of scientific studies to back it up . . . but if the scientific community will not study it, this ensures that there cannot be much scientific evidence about it!

NLP has helped me to overwrite many of the unhelpful and limiting beliefs that I grew up with.

Part of the problem with NLP, apart from the fact that it has not been embraced scientifically, is that it's a field that has generally lacked a professional association that might hold practitioners to a proper standard. It has also been incorporated into many personal-development courses that have in some cases diluted and altered the original teachings, devolving into quackery in some cases. Hence, it's important to know the integrity of the source material you are using and, if using an NLP practitioner, to ensure that he or she really does have the proper qualifications and experience.

Robert Dilts and Tim Hallbom are both highly experienced and were trained personally by the founders of NLP. Earlier in this chapter I referred to a book that they coauthored, and also to an excellent workshop conducted by Tim Hallbom and his partner, Kris Hallbom, that specifically addresses money and wealth beliefs called *The WealthyMind Program*. That workshop is available on DVD from www.thewealthymind.com, and it contains instruction on an excellent belief-change protocol that you can do at home, either by yourself or with a friend to help you.

7. Cognitive Behavior Therapy (CBT)

Cognitive behavior therapy, which I discussed at the beginning of this book, has more support from the scientific community than NLP does. CBT is quite widely practiced in psychotherapeutic circles and has a significant number of scientific efficacy studies that back it up as a valuable and effective therapeutic technique.[8]

Cognitive therapy (CT), the predecessor of CBT, was described in the late 1960s by American psychiatrist Aaron T. Beck, as I previously discussed. The technique focused on examining previously unquestioned beliefs and using the cognitive (thinking) mind to question their validity.

Sound familiar? This is pretty much what we have been doing in the preceding chapters by looking critically at each of the 7 Money Myths as a key step in programming your *Abundance Code*.

Cognitive behavior therapy has been successfully applied to a wide range of psychological disorders.

Later, especially in the 1980s and '90s, it was recognized that the efficacy of cognitive therapy could be enhanced by adding into the therapeutic mix several behavior-modification and conditioning techniques, such as the classical conditioning technique developed by Ivan Pavlov (familiar to many through the famous Pavlov's dog experiment) and the operant conditioning technique developed by B. F. Skinner. This expanded therapeutic protocol came to be known as cognitive behavior therapy.

CBT has been successfully applied to a wide range of psychological disorders, including depression, anxiety disorders, post-traumatic stress disorder, insomnia, eating disorders, and various substance addictions.

As with any type of psychotherapy, it is important to seek out an appropriately qualified and certified practitioner.

Keep on Reaching for Those Bananas!

So now you have seven different tools in your toolbox that you can use for the important (and life-transforming) task of money myth busting. I would argue that the 7 Money Myths that I have described in this book are powerful cultural myths, so the task of *myth busting* is not to be undertaken lightly. The job of overwriting these powerful beliefs should be approached with willingness, perseverance, and a certain sense of humility. This book has provided you with a road map for changing your beliefs so that you can access greater levels of abundance and freedom in your life.

Remember the monkey story I related at the beginning of this chapter? Well, if you want to reach the bananas, once you have shifted your own mind-set to believe that it's actually possible to get them, you may still have to take a beating from some brainwashed monkeys in the process.

You're going to need the courage of your convictions, but the reward will be worth it. Keep trying and you'll figure it out. When you do, you'll get that bunch of bananas, and you might just show those other monkeys how it's done, too.

If at first you don't succeed on your path to financial freedom, try, try again!

Digging Deep

1. What are some habitual behaviors you have that you might like to change?

2. What beliefs do you think might be driving these unwanted habits? Sometimes this is not the easiest thing to figure out, but try asking yourself the following questions to help shed some light: When was the first time you started the habit? What were you feeling at the time? Had anything significant just happened in your life?

3. What are some positive habits you would like to establish?

4. How can an understanding of the habit loop assist you in forming new habits?

Action Steps

1. Try the sleepy-mind or relaxation method first. These are great places to start, and there's no time like the present. Try one of them tonight! Remember to check that your new belief statement is well formed, using the checklist in this chapter, and explore what it will feel like to have that outcome in your life.

2. Make a vision board. Cut out pictures from magazines and newspapers or download images online and arrange them on a sheet of cardboard or poster board. Cut out words or simple phrases as well to put with the images. Once you have everything you want arranged on the board, glue it all in place and hang your vision board somewhere you'll be able to see it multiple times a day.

3. If you really want to go deep on reprogramming your mind regarding wealth, do Tim Hallbom and Kris Hallbom's *The WealthyMind Program*. (And no, I don't get a commission for saying that!) It really is a very good DVD program, taking you through a powerful process to install more supportive beliefs about money, success, and wealth. It's not very expensive, and in my opinion it's some of the best money you will ever spend.

AFTERWORD

I see the 7 Money Myths a bit like a set of belief hurdles that have been put between you and your attainment of abundant wealth, freedom, and choice. Your *Abundance Code* is the programming you proactively install in your mind instead of these barriers, the programming that brings you to a place of freedom.

Another way of looking at it is that unlocking your wealth potential is like unlocking a series of doors in your mind, doors that lead you out of the mental prison of scarcity—or Scare-City—and into the wonderful mental playground of possibility that I call the Abundance Forest.

Now, you may have noticed that I placed the 7 Money Myths in a particular sequence in the book, so let me take a moment to explain why I did that.

Imagine you are an innocent and inquisitive child—you know, the kind of child who always asks "Why?" when presented with some so-called fact about the world, who often asks "Why not?" when they are told no, and who loves to wonder "What if?" And imagine that, as this child, someone told you that you can't have all the things that you want.

"What?!"

Once you've finished throwing your toys out of your pram, what's the first question you might ask?

"Why not?"

"Because," you are told, "there's not enough to go around, so sometimes you have to go without."

You've just hit the first mental barrier: scarcity.

Being the inquisitive child that you are, that doesn't stop you from asking more questions.

"So if I want to have more, what do I need to do?"

"Well, you have to work. You have to work hard, and you have to work long. You have to work harder and longer than others if you want to have more."

You've now hit the second mental barrier (*time = money*), but you're still asking questions.

"Surely there's a limit to how long I can work. Isn't there any other way that I can get more?"

"There is one way, but for that your work has to be worth more than that of others."

You've just hit the third barrier (*work = worth*).

"But what if there's a limit to how much an hour of my time is going to be worth?" I hear you ask. "What else can I do to get more?"

"Unless you already have a bunch of money, there's not much else you can do. It takes money to make money if you don't want to work hard for it."

That's the fourth barrier (it takes money to make money).

"Okay. But let's say I do get some money, then will more money come to me easily?"

"Ha! You want a shortcut, do you? Well, good luck, because for most people, it's easy come, easy go. Money in, money out. Only people with money know-how are able to hang onto it."

You've hit the fifth barrier (easy come, easy go), and at this point you have an Aha! moment. You feel that you are getting close to cracking this puzzle.

So you say, "What if I learn about money? What if I get the know-how? Then will I finally be able to get what I want?"

"Maybe," you are told. "But trust me—it won't make you happy, so you might as well not bother."

That's the sixth barrier (money won't make you happy) . . . but by this stage you're getting a little suspicious of the answers you're hearing.

"Hang on," you say. "I think that money might not make me *un*happy. I'm going to go for it!"

"Well! Do so at your own risk . . . because if you succeed and get a lot of money, your soul will probably be corrupted by it. It will end badly for you—if not in this life, then in the next."

And that is the seventh barrier (money will corrupt you).

Hopefully at this point you'll retort with something like, "Yeah, right. Whatever! I don't believe you," and then merrily continue on your way to the Abundance Forest!

And once you get there . . . well, everything opens up. Everything is possible. The only limitations are the ones you allow to remain in your own mind.

Beliefs *Are* Powerful Things

This book has been about both examining and changing your beliefs about money and making sure that your subconscious beliefs—your *Abundance Code*—align with your conscious goals for wealth, success, and financial freedom.

It is critically important to realize that you *can* be successful and you *can* be wealthy. You *can* make money without expending physical effort or time. You *can* become financially free, with an abundance of money and freedom of choice. It's all possible for you, if you *believe*.

Let's review some of the key points we have covered in this book about money beliefs:

- Desire and knowledge alone are not enough. You also need a set of supporting subconscious beliefs in order to be able to attain your desires.

- Desire + Knowledge + Belief = Success

- Desire + Knowledge – Belief = Frustration

- It's possible that humans are wired in an evolutionary sense to give more weight to negative news, to operate from fear, and to believe in scarcity. But scarcity is not a fact. You can reprogram yourself to be more optimistic; to believe in abundance; and to operate from a position of generosity, hope, and possibility.

- You can escape the constraint of exchanging your time for money. It's possible to get your money to work for you, making you more money and allowing you to access more freedom and abundance in your life.

- Your work does not define your worth. You define your worth.

- You don't need to have a lot of money to start with, but you may need to start getting your money to work *for you* if you want to eventually free yourself financially.

- Money can come to you easily, without your always having to work hard for it or exchange your time for it, and it can stick around to make even more money for you.

- Money can support and facilitate your quest for a happier and more fulfilling life.

- Money does not corrupt people; mind-set corrupts people. You can have money *and* have a generous, abundant, uncorrupted mind-set.

- Supportive and positive beliefs about money are critical to ensuring your ultimate success. Once you have established a supportive set of beliefs about money, experience (the new habit loop) is the only teacher that can really drive the message home and reinforce your new beliefs.

So let's look at the practical implementation of these ideas— the installation and ignition of your *Abundance Code*. There are certain steps that you will have to take along the road to financial freedom:

- Take the time to examine your beliefs about money and financial abundance.

- Ensure that your beliefs about money are in alignment with your goals for financial freedom.

- If your beliefs are not in alignment, change them.

- Pay attention to the habit loop and apply the golden rule of habit change to help adjust your behavior patterns around money.

- Take the time to acquire some knowledge about wealth-creation techniques.

- Begin setting aside an amount of capital that you will use in order to put wealth-creation techniques into practice for yourself.

- Learn to manage your emotions regarding money— that is, learn to conquer both greed and fear.

- Allow yourself to experience a learning curve. This means viewing your mistakes as valuable learning experiences and not getting too cocky about your successes.

- Keep at it and don't give up!

If I had to sum the whole process up into three simple steps, I would say this:

1. Do the vital belief-change work to get your subconscious beliefs in alignment with your conscious desires.

2. Stay awake and aware, always vigilant for the signs of subconscious sabotage.

3. Do your best, let experience be your guide, and use the habit loop to your advantage.

There is a Chinese proverb, often attributed to Confucius, that says, "I hear and I forget. I see and I remember. I do and I understand." When it comes to financial freedom, once you really "get it" on the inside, both consciously and subconsciously, then you'll *get it* . . . meaning you'll attain it on the outside.

It is my sincere hope that this book helps you on your path to attaining true and lasting financial freedom. I know you can.

And why do I know that?

Because . . . *I believe.*

ENDNOTES

CHAPTER 2

1. Jonathan J. Koehler, "The Influence of Prior Beliefs on Scientific Judgments of Evidence Quality," *Organizational Behavior & Human Decision Processes* 56 (1993): 28.

2. Raymond S. Nickerson, "Confirmation Bias; A Ubiquitous Phenomenon in Many Guises," *Review of General Psychology* 2, no. 2 (1998): 175–220; Ziva Kunda, *Social Cognition: Making Sense of People* (MIT Press, 1999).

3. "Cognitive Therapy," *Wikipedia,* http://en.wikipedia.org/wiki/Cognitive_therapy.

CHAPTER 3

1. Peter H. Diamandis and Steven Kotler, *Abundance: The Future Is Better Than You Think* (New York: Free Press, 2012).

2. One great source of inspiring videos about progress and innovation is TED: www.ted.com.

3. To see this demonstrated, check out a great TED presentation Hans Rosling gave in 2006: "The Best Stats You've Ever Seen," filmed February 2006, TED video, 19:50, www.ted.com/talks/lang/en/hans_rosling_shows_the_best_stats_you_ve_ever_seen.html.

4. Check out some more of Hans Rosling's TED talks, such as this more recent one: "Let My Dataset Change Your Mindset," filmed June 2009, TED video, 19:56, http://www.ted.com/talks/hans_rosling_at_state.html.

5. Please note that if you are suffering from depression, bipolar disorder, or any form of mental illness or condition, or are on medication for any mental health conditions, you should consult your mental health advisor before beginning any program of meditation.

CHAPTER 4

1. Lily Altavena, "One in Two New College Graduates Is Jobless or Underemployed," *The Choice* (blog), *New York Times*, April 27, 2012, http://thechoice.blogs.nytimes.com/2012/04/27/one-in-two-new-college-graduates-i-jobless-or-underemployed/.

CHAPTER 5

1. Robert Kiyosaki with Sharon L. Lechter, CPA, *Rich Dad's Prophecy: Why the Biggest Stock Market Crash in History Is Still Coming . . . and How You Can Prepare Yourself and Profit from It!* (New York: Warner Books, 2002).

2. Ibid.

CHAPTER 6

1. Jennifer Skattebol, Peter Saunders, Gerry Redmond, Megan Bedford, and Bettina Cass, "Making a Difference: Building on Young People's Experiences of Economic Adversity," Social Policy Research Centre Report Series (Sydney, NSW: University of New South Wales, August 2012).

CHAPTER 7

1. Scott Hankins, Mark Hoekstra, and Paige Marta Skiba, "The Ticket to Easy Street? The Financial Consequences of Winning the Lottery," *The Review of Economics and Statistics* 93, no. 3 (August 2011).

2. H. Roy Kaplan, "The Social and Economic Impact of State Lotteries," *Annals of the American Academy of Political and Social Science* 474 (July 1984); "$325 Million: Big Win, Big Problems?" *Gaming Magazine*, April 17, 2002, http://web.archive.org/web/20070220225859/http://www.gamingmagazine.com/managearticle.asp?c=220&a=1156.

3. Robert Frank, "Will Winning the Lottery Ruin Your Life?" *The Wealth Report* (blog), *Wall Street Journal*, March 30, 2012, http://blogs.wsj.com/wealth/2012/03/30/will-winning-the-lottery-ruin-your-life/.

4. "Cambridge Neuroscientist Dr. John Coates Publishes New Book on the Biology of Risk Taking," Cambridge Neuroscience, University of Cambridge, May 15, 2012, http://www.neuroscience.cam.ac.uk/news/article.php?permalink=3feea350b9.

5. James Pressley, "Goldman-Bred Neuroscientist Tracks Testosterone Trading," *Bloomberg Business*, May 13, 2012, http://www.bloomberg.com/news/2012-05-13/goldman-bred-neuroscientist-bares-secret-of-testosterone-trading.html.

CHAPTER 8

1. Lara B. Aknin, Michael I. Norton, and Elizabeth W. Dunn, "From Wealth to Well-being? Money Matters, but Less Than People Think," *Journal of Positive Psychology* 4, no. 6 (November 2009).

2. Skattebol et al., "Making a Difference . . ."

3. Paul Taylor, Cary Funk, and Peyton Craighill, "Are We Happy Yet?" Social Trends Report, Pew Research Center, February 13, 2006, http://pewsocialtrends.org/files/2010/10/AreWeHappyYet.pdf.

4. David Leonhardt, "Maybe Money Does Buy Happiness After All," *New York Times,* April 16, 2008, http://www.nytimes.com/2008/04/16/business/16leonhardt.html?.

5. Betsey Stevenson and Justin Wolfers, "Economic Growth and Subjective Well-Being: Reassessing the Easterlin Paradox," *Brookings Papers on Economic Activity* 39, no. 1 (2008).

6. Elizabeth W. Dunn, Lara B. Aknin, and Michael I. Norton, "Spending Money on Others Promotes Happiness," *Science* 319, no 5870 (March 21, 2008): 1687–1688.

7. Karma Currency website, www.karmacurrency.com.au.

8. Taylor et al., "Are We Happy Yet?"

9. A. H. Maslow, "A Theory of Human Motivation," *Psychological Review* 50, no. 4 (July 1943): 370–396.

10. Tal Ben-Shahar, Ph.D., *Happier: Learn the Secrets to Daily Joy and Lasting Fulfillment* (New York: McGraw-Hill, 2007).

CHAPTER 9

1. 1 Tim. 6:10 (New International Version)

2. Mark 10:25 (NIV)

3. Mark 8:36 (NIV)

4. Mark 10:21 (NIV)

5. Mark 10:26 (NIV)

6. Mark 10:27 (NIV)

7. Notes accompanying Mark 10:21, NIV Study Bible (1984), 1514.

8. Mark 10:15 (NIV)

9. Norman Doidge, M.D., *The Brain That Changes Itself: Stories of Personal Triumph from the Frontiers of Brain Science* (New York: Viking Penguin, 2007).

10. Ed Diener and Eunkook Suh, "Measuring Quality of Life: Economic, Social, and Subjective Indicators." *Social Indicators Research* 40, no. 1–2 (1997): 189–216.

11. Purchasing power per capita is a measure that normalizes the incomes of citizens in a given country so that valid cross-country comparisons can be made.

12. Stephen D. Levitt, "The Changing Relationship Between Income and Crime Victimization," *Federal Reserve Bank of New York Economic Policy Review* (September 1999).

13. Michael I. Norton and Dan Ariely, "Building a Better America—One Wealth Quintile at a Time," *Perspectives on Psychological Science* 6, no. 1 (January 2011): 9–12.

14. For a great video representation of these research findings, see "Wealth Inequality in America," YouTube video, 6:23, posted by "politizane," November 20, 2012, http://www.youtube.com/watch?v=QPKKQnijnsM.

CHAPTER 10

1. Michael Basilico, "Five Monkeys," Vimeo video, 1:25, http://vimeo.com/32948807.

2. Tim Hallbom and Kris Hallbom, *The WealthyMind Program Workbook* (2009).

3. Charles Duhigg, *The Power of Habit: Why We Do What We Do and How to Change* (New York: Random House, 2012).

4. Ibid.

5. Ibid.

6. Ibid.

7. This technique is similar to that described as the "Baudoin technique" in *The Power of Your Subconscious Mind* by Joseph Murphy.

8. A. C. Butler, J. E. Chapman, E. M. Forman, and A. T. Beck, "The Empirical Status of Cognitive Behavioral Therapy: A Review of Meta-analyses," *Clinical Psychology Review* 26, no. 1(2006): 17–31.

ACKNOWLEDGMENTS

I would like to thank my longtime friend and mentor Nitya Amrita, who spent many hours with me over the past decade discussing the ideas behind this book, helping me refine the concepts, and even co-delivering a weekend workshop with me on the topic. In truth, this book would not exist without her valuable input and insights. My friend Marlo Slavin pointed me toward some interesting background material, for which I am grateful.

I would also like to thank the hundreds of Elite Coaching clients from my business in Australia, Trading Pursuits, who read earlier drafts of this book and provided valuable feedback. Thanks also to topic experts Jill Pleban; Lindsay Duncan, Ph.D.; and Ruth Buczynski, Ph.D., for reading previous drafts and providing some very insightful comments and suggestions. And my eternal gratitude to my trusty editor Georgina Bible, who went over my original manuscript several times with a deft hand for flow and an eagle eye for detail. And to the Hay House editors Jessica Kelley, Alex Freemon, Lindsay DiGianvittorio, and Celeste Phillips, who helped me restructure the manuscript in a way that made a lot more sense.

Thanks to Daniel Kertcher, my business partner, friend, former husband, and co-parent to our wonderful daughter, Chantal. Thank you both for supporting me and for believing in me, always, without fail.

Thanks to my family and my friends for listening to me endlessly talk about this project, for reading drafts, and for cheering me on.

Thanks to the amazing mastermind group Jeff Walker founded in 2010, of which I have had the outstanding privilege to be a member since its inception. The positive influence of being surrounded by like-minded people who are all focused on creating incredible value and abundance in their lives and in the world is something that I did not fully understand the importance of when I began this journey. I do now. To every member of that group, and especially to Jeff Walker and his team, I wish to express my heartfelt gratitude.

To my wonderful business coach and mentor Mark Falzon—you inspire me to step up again and again into being the best version of myself that I can envision. And to my beloved spiritual teacher Amma—there simply are no words that can adequately express what your loving guidance, profound presence, and wisdom have meant in my life. You have inspired me to get past my own perceived "smallness," to seek a way to give back to the world from my abundance, and to be of service to my fellow travelers.

And finally, thanks to Louise Hay for writing her inspiring book *You Can Heal Your Life*. Once upon a time in my very early 20s, when my life did not feel as abundant to me as it does now . . . when I found myself in a very dark place, wasn't very keen on living, and didn't know quite how to dig my way out of that hole . . . Louise Hay's book made all the difference to me. For that reason and many others, I feel so honored, blessed, and grateful, to have the privilege of becoming a Hay House author.

ABOUT THE AUTHOR

Julie Ann Cairns has been the co-owner and managing director of Trading Pursuits Group, a financial-markets education company established in 2001. She has built her own personal wealth through investing in the stock market, real estate, and entrepreneurial business ventures.

Julie Ann believes in inspiring others to transform themselves and their lives through practical financial wisdom supported by a wealthy mind-set so that they can achieve personal and financial freedom. Her life mission is to empower people to live an abundant life free from limiting beliefs.

Website: www.julieanncairns.com

We hope you enjoyed this Hay House book.
If you'd like to receive our online catalog featuring additional
information on Hay House books and products,
or if you'd like to find out more about the
Hay Foundation, please contact:

Hay House, Inc., P.O. Box 5100, Carlsbad, CA 92018-5100
(760) 431-7695 or (800) 654-5126
(760) 431-6948 (fax) or (800) 650-5115 (fax)
www.hayhouse.com® • www.hayfoundation.org

Published and distributed in Australia by: Hay House Australia Pty. Ltd.,
18/36 Ralph St., Alexandria NSW 2015
Phone: 612-9669-4299 • *Fax:* 612-9669-4144 • www.hayhouse.com.au

Published and distributed in the United Kingdom by: Hay House UK, Ltd.,
Astley House, 33 Notting Hill Gate, London W11 3JQ
Phone: 44-20-3675-2450 • *Fax:* 44-20-3675-2451 • www.hayhouse.co.uk

Published and distributed in the Republic of South Africa by:
Hay House SA (Pty), Ltd., P.O. Box 990, Witkoppen 2068
info@ hayhouse.co.za • www.hayhouse.co.za

Published in India by: Hay House Publishers India,
Muskaan Complex, Plot No. 3, B-2, Vasant Kunj, New Delhi 110 070
Phone: 91-11-4176-1620 • *Fax:* 91-11-4176-1630 • www.hayhouse.co.in

Distributed in Canada by: Raincoast Books,
2440 Viking Way, Richmond, B.C. V6V 1N2
Phone: 1-800-663-5714 • *Fax:* 1-800-565-3770 • www.raincoast.com

Take Your Soul on a Vacation
Visit www.HealYourLife.com® to regroup, recharge,
and reconnect with your own magnificence.
Featuring blogs, mind-body-spirit news, and
life-changing wisdom from Louise Hay and friends.
Visit www.HealYourLife.com today!